THE PEOPLE OF THE BOOK

Other volumes in this series:

The People of the Way: The Story Behind the New Testament
The People of the Creed: The Story Behind the Early Church
Further volumes in preparation.

Also by Anthony E. Gilles:

Fundamentalism: What Every Catholic Needs to Know
Getting Acquainted With the New Testament (a cassette series)
Getting Acquainted With the Early Church (a cassette series)
Fundamentalism Today: A Catholic Response (a cassette series)

THE
PEOPLE
OF THE
BOOK

The Story Behind the Old Testament

ANTHONY E. GILLES

Nihil Obstat:	Rev. Hilarion Kistner, O.F.M.
	Rev. John J. Jennings
Imprimi Potest:	Rev. Jeremy Harrington, O.F.M.
	Provincial
Imprimatur:	Rev. John L. Cavanaugh, V.G.
	Archdiocese of Cincinnati
	July 8, 1983

Unless otherwise indicated, Scripture texts are excerpts from *The Jerusalem Bible,* copyright © 1966 by Darton, Longman & Todd, Ltd., and Doubleday & Company, Inc. Used by permission of the publisher.

Book design and cover by Julie Lonneman

SBN 0-86716-026-8

To Thomas Keating, O.C.S.O.,
AND
Matthew Torpey, O.C.S.O.

PREFACE

During my childhood my devout Catholic parents kept a large family Bible on permanent display in a corner of our living room. It was always there, and we children could turn its pages whenever we chose. No one ever *encouraged* us to do so, but from time to time I would thumb through the pages and look at the glossy pictures of Daniel in the lion's den or the long-haired Samson poised to pull down the pillars of the Philistine temple.

I marveled at the bulk of information compressed into that one volume, and marveled as well at how wise my pastor must be for having the ability to understand such a mystifying book. It never entered my mind that I would one day come to understand the Bible for myself. It certainly never occurred to me that I would ever teach courses on Scripture or write a book about the subject.

In my home, as I suspect was the situation in most pre-Vatican II Catholic homes, we received our education in Scripture from the readings at Sunday Mass. This was a sound method of instruction for some people. I am still amazed at the amount my parents learned from simply listening to the Bible being read, while reading it very rarely themselves. That they were able to absorb the message of Scripture and put it into effect so evidently in their lives proved to me that the old way of doing things worked—at least for some of the older Catholics.

I found, however, that *I* needed something more than the old method of learning Scripture. Passage through the turmoil of the 60's and the near-revolution in Catholicism wrought by Vatican II brought me haphazardly to my 28th year. Searching one day for spiritual counsel through the shelves of a large book store in Atlanta, and jaded by the scores of books on "inner enlightenment" which I had already studied, I suddenly realized that I had never really read the Bible for myself. I picked one off the shelf, opened it at random and read, "The kingdom of heaven is among you" (Lk 17:21). I had been coming to that same conclusion for myself already, and wondered what else the Bible might have to say on the subject. This desire motivated me to buy my first Bible.

That first weekend—extending from Friday afternoon until 2 a.m. Monday morning—I read from "In the beginning..." to "*Maranatha*" without skipping a single word in between. During that summer I read the entire Bible two more times in sequence, from start to finish. By September I felt like a blind man who had swung a pick and shovel all day in a rich diamond mine: I knew I had discovered something, but I didn't know what it was. I realized I needed help.

I soon discovered there is probably more written on the Bible than on any other subject, and I proceeded to read as much of it as I could. Gradually, the background of the biblical landscape started to come into focus. I then read all the English versions of Scripture and settled on the *Jerusalem Bible* as the one I would stick with for a while. Finally, I sought out—and stumbled across—the scholarly experts on the Bible, and pursued them through classrooms, seminaries and monasteries until I had my answers. I discovered that the more I learned the more unfathomable my subject became, but at least I was starting to define the boundaries of my ignorance.

It is now nine years after the start of my adventure, and I find that Scripture is for me an ever-deepening cavern of treasures. One night not long ago, upon the conclusion of one of the adult Bible classes which I teach, the last person in a heartwarmingly long line of grateful students told me, "You ought to write a book on the Bible for people just like us."

"Are you kidding?" I asked her. "You can't get Catholics to take seriously anything a lay person writes about the Bible. It's hard enough to get them to read what priests and nuns write!"

My friend rejected my half sarcastic, half self-pitying response and pressed her point.

"You ought to try anyway," she said. "This is the first time in my life I've really understood the Bible. You really opened up the subject for me."

To make a long story short, a few more remarks like that during the following weeks from former students won me over. I put pen to paper, and you are now reading (and I hope will continue reading) the finished product.

My purpose in writing this book is to introduce the ordinary Catholic—someone who has neither the time nor the training to read a lengthy, academic treatise—to a deeper knowledge of the Bible. (I hope that a Protestant brother or sister or two will take a peek also, if for no other reason than to discover that we Catholics are finally getting serious about reading the Bible!)

This book is limited to the Old Testament (although I hope to follow shortly with a volume on the New Testament). I hope this present volume will inspire people to undertake or extend their own adventure in scriptural exploration.

This study is intended only as a guidebook for travel to the kingdom of the Word. You should keep in mind that while guidebooks are fun to look at, travel to the actual country is much more exciting. Therefore, as you read this book, I encourage you to stop every now and then to get to know the Old Testament on its own terms, for yourself.

—Anthony E. Gilles

CONTENTS

INTRODUCTION

This is a book about how the old Testament came to be written. The "book" we call the Old Testament is actually a collection of *several* books, written at different times, by different authors, from varying perspectives. It would be impossible to understand how the unified collection came into existence without first understanding how each book which makes up the collection was written.

To achieve this understanding we will proceed according to the following plan: First, we will separate the different books out from the whole. Second, we will investigate the historical context out of which each book arose.

Since we will be taking an historical approach, we must begin at the beginning—the beginning of the history of "the People of the Book," the Jewish people who gave us the Old Testament. What is that beginning? Is there one moment or event which we can point to as having definitively molded the ancestors of the Jews into a nation based on shared religious and social values?

There is such an event, and it is called the *Exodus*. We will define the Exodus as the sequence of episodes which began with the Hebrews' escape from Egypt, their miraculous crossing of the Sea of Reeds (Red Sea) and their entering into a covenant with Yahweh at Mt. Sinai.

Before the Exodus event it would be incorrect to say that there was an Israelite history in the strict sense. The ancient stories of the patriarchs which are recorded in Genesis might be better called *prehistory*. (That is why we will begin *our* study with the Exodus event, described in the Biblical book that bears the same name, rather than with Genesis.)

These stories were based on real historical figures and real occurrences. Yet the stories were of no significance to the development of the Old Testament until there was a people who could reflect on them and determine their value to the ongoing life of the community.

Perhaps the following illustration will make this abstract idea clearer. At the time of Abraham, about 1800 B.C., there were a number of nomadic tribes similar to his living in the same region. Yet, we know next to nothing about the family histories of these other tribes. Why? Simply because nothing of enough importance ever happened to these other tribes to form them into a community possessing a consciousness of their past.

These other tribes simply died off, were conquered and assimilated, or otherwise merged into other communities of people. Years later, no one ever thought to write down all those old stories about "way back when" because there was no community in existence at that point to *remember* "way back when."

With Abraham's tribe it was different. His tribe didn't die out. Instead it flourished, and descendants of that tribe eventually formed themselves into a new nation. At *that point* the earlier stories about Abraham became significant. *Then* the descendants of Abraham could say, "It looks like we've really got something going here. We'd better write down those old stories about Abraham and the boys before we forget them."

The important point is that some historical event had to bring Abraham's descendants to a level of development where they found they *needed* to write a history of their early ancestry. That something was the Exodus event. It is because the Exodus event had such a catalytic effect in the development of the Israelite nation that we start this book there rather than with Genesis.

There is one final point to consider. It concerns the authors of the various Old Testament books we will be considering. Since the art of writing during the time under consideration was much more primitive than it is today, authors of the Old Testament books followed different conventions than we do. For one thing, they didn't sign their names to anything they wrote. As a result, we know the authors' names for only a very few of the Old Testament books.

Neither were there copyright laws back then; the concept of plagiarism was nonexistent. The purpose of writing was to enchance the life of the community, not to glorify the author's name or earn a living as is often the purpose today. Consequently, we will often find books of the Old Testament stitched together from several "sources," not written by one person only.

A "source" is simply a tradition or story concerning an event or person which an Old Testament author used in putting together the finished product. These sources were both oral and written. The earliest sources were, of course, oral. They gradually came to be written down in rudimentary form, and were incorporated into later written sources, and eventually into the particular Old Testament book as we know it today.

We don't know all of the sources which were used in the writing of the Old Testament, but we do know some of the most important ones. Since, as I have said, authors' names were not used, scholars have had to invent names to go with the various sources. You will come across the four most famous of these sources—and their common abbreviations—during the course of reading this book: *Yahwist* (J), *Elohist* (E), *Deuteronomist* (D) and *Priestly* (P). At one place in the book I offer my own abbreviations for two lesser known sources, which I call "G" and "B." Other sources have more ordinary names, such as "The Court History of King David" referred to in Chapter Five.

If this is the first time you've encountered this information on sources it may be a bit confusing to you. The following analogy might help you understand how the sources contributed to the finished product of the Old Testament as we have it today.

Suppose you were commissioned by your relatives to write a family history. How would you proceed? You would probably go back and collect as many bits and pieces of information as you could before you started writing. You would talk to Grandma, who would tell you stories about her childhood. She might even remember stories about *her* grandmother's childhood—which could extend back as far as 150 years. Next, you would look at Aunt Kate's old diaries and Uncle Herman's letters, particularly the ones he wrote home during World War II. You might even use an old recipe for a section on your family's favorite dish. Or you might look up newspaper clippings in the town where your Grandpa was born.

All of these materials are *sources*. Some of them are oral and some written. You are the one who has to weave them together into the family history. Perhaps you write your first draft in longhand. Next Cousin Ernie comes along and types it, correcting your grammar and syntax as he does so. Then, to top it off, rich Uncle Dave decides the manuscript is so valuable to the family that he wants to have it printed in a leather cover. He even hires an editor to make it read as though it were a professionally written history.

The important thing to notice here is that the starting point for the finished product at each stage of development was the original sources you collected. The Old Testament was written in pretty much the same way. As the family history of God's chosen people, it owes its existence to the sources on which it is based.

I hope this analogy will help you in the chapters ahead. We will trace the "family history" of God's people and identify the sources which helped to shape it. Most importantly of all, we will gain insights into the God who called and continues to call that family into relationship with him.

TABLE OF SCRIPTURE ABBREVIATION

Acts—Acts of the Apostles
Am—Amos
Bar—Baruch
1 Chr—1 Chronicles
2 Chr—2 Chronicles
Col—Colossians
1 Cor—1 Corinthians
2 Cor—2 Corinthians
Dn—Daniel
Dt—Deuteronomy
Eccl—Ecclesiastes
Eph—Ephesians
Est—Esther
Ex—Exodus
Ez—Ezekiel
Ezr—Ezra
Gal—Galatians
Gn—Genesis
Hb—Habakkuk
Heb—Hebrews
Hg—Haggai
Hos—Hosea
Is—Isaiah
Jas—James
Jb—Job
Jdt—Judith
Jer—Jeremiah
Jl—Joel
Jgs—Judges
Jn—John
1 Jn—1 John
2 Jn—2 John
3 Jn—3 John
Jon—Jonah
Jos—Joshua
Jude—Jude
1 Kgs—1 Kings
2 Kgs—2 Kings
Lam—Lamentations
Lk—Luke
Lv— Leviticus
Mal—Malachi
1 Mc—1 Maccabees
2 Mc—2 Maccabees
Mi—Micah

Mk—Mark
Mt—Matthew
Na—Nahum
Neh—Nehem
Nm—Number
Ob—Obadiah
1 Pt—1 Peter
2 Pt—2 Peter
Phil—Philippians
Phlm—Philemon
Prv—Proverbs
Ps—Psalms
Rom—Romans
Ru—Ruth
Rv—Revelation
Song—Song of Songs
Sir—Ecclesiasticus (Sirach)
1 Sm—1 Samuel
2 Sm—2 Samuel
Tb— Tobit
1 Thes—1 Thessalonians
2 Thes—2 Thessalonians
Ti—Titus
1 Tm—1 Timothy
2 Tm—2 Timothy
Wis—Wisdom
Zec—Zechariah
Zep—Zephaniah

Stages in Biblical Writing

Oral traditions, folk tales, stories of the patriarchs circulate among clans and tr[...] (Some perhaps committed to writing in rudimentary form.)

Oral tales of the Exodus and life in the desert circulate. (Some perhaps committed to writing in rudimentary form.)

Gilgal Account (G), Boundary Setter (B), Song of Deborah (Jgs 5) committed to writing.

J combines old tales and scraps of prior writing—the beginnings of Gn, Ex, Nm; Ps, Prv begin to develop. The Court History of David. Sources of 1 and 2 Sm. Origins of Song of Songs, Ruth.

The schism of 931 hardens the distinction between northern and southern traditions. Each shapes the old tales according to respective interests.

The Elijah and Elisha Cycles. Sources for 1 and 2 Kgs take shape. E begins work in the north.

Prophetic schools in north committed to writing: Am, Hos.

J-E tradition: E brought south by devout Yahwists to merge with J.

Prophetic writing in Judah: Compilation of writings associated with Isaiah of Jerusalem. Mi. Zep.

The D school. Origins of Dt.

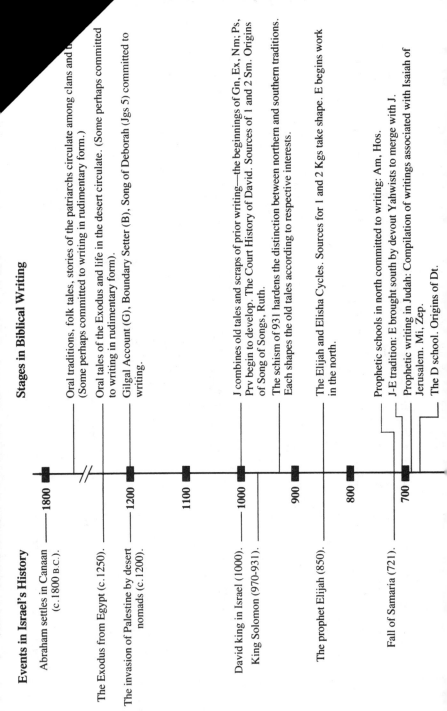

Events in Israel's History

Abraham settles in Canaan (c. 1800 B.C.).

The Exodus from Egypt (c. 1250).

The invasion of Palestine by desert nomads (c. 1200).

David king in Israel (1000).

King Solomon (970-931).

The prophet Elijah (850).

Fall of Samaria (721).

1800

1200

1100

1000

900

800

700

Na, Hb, the early Jer. Origins of D history in Jos-Kgs: Joshua to Josiah (1200-622).

The later Jer, the early Ez. Israel's oral and written traditions carried to Babylon.

Exilic writings: the later Ez; P school begins editing. Holiness Code worked into Lv. P, using J-E, writes first edition of "tetrateuch" (Gn, Ex, Lv, Nm). Final D-editor completes Jos-Kgs history (to 562). Second-Isaiah. Wisdom literature integrates Exile experience.

Restoration writing: Zec, Hg, Mal, Ob, Jl, "Second Zechariah," Jb. The Chronicler finishes 1 and 2 Chr, Ez and Neh. P adds D's work to "tetrateuch" and finishes first edition of Pentateuch. Jon, Eccl.

Dn 1—6, Est and Tb written in Ptolemaic period (323-220). The P school further edits Pentateuch. Rabbis discuss canonicity. Jos-Kgs history, prophetic works refined and edited.

Jewish Resistance Literature: 1 and 2 Mc, Dn 7—12, Jdt. Around 180: Sir.

Wis written in Alexandria. Rabbis debate contents of Jewish Scriptures.

At Council of Jamnia, canon of Jewish Scriptures is closed. Jewish Bible divided into "law" and "prophets." Greek works excluded, as well as recent Hebrew works.

---

600 — 500 — 400 — 300 — 200 — 100 — 100

Josiah's reform (622).

Fall of Jerusalem, the Exile (587).

Return of the exiles to Jerusalem (538).

Careers of Ezra and Nehemiah (c. 450).

Alexander the Great. Greek control of Palestine begins (333-323).

Antiochus Epiphanes becomes king in Palestine (175).

The Maccabean revolt (168).

The Romans supplant the Greeks in the east; descendants of the Maccabees rule Palestine as high priests (64). Struggles between Sadducees, Pharisees.

Birth of Christ (4 B.C.).

Meeting of rabbis at Jamnia (90 A.D.).

CHAPTER ONE

'ON EAGLES' WINGS'

Exodus

You live in the Egyptian Delta during the reign of Pharaoh Rameses II. It is the second half of the 13th century before Christ. You are part of the vast body of migrants whose ancestors wandered into Egypt years, decades, even centuries before. *Apiru*. That is the name by which you hear Pharaoh's foremen refer to you and your people. *Apiru*. A people who don't seem to have come from anywhere in particular and don't seem to have any true homeland to which to return. But you are different.

You take pride in being a special type of *Apiru*. There is an ancient story which circulates in your clan. It is a marvelous, fascinating story which is told over and over again at campfires when night edges in on your people's settlement. An old, bearded wise man tells it best.

Once there was a prime minister in Egypt—an *Apiru*—who ruled the entire land as if he were Pharaoh's very brother. This man, the story goes, had 11 brothers. The father of these 12 brothers was named Israel. You are descended from that family of 12 brothers and you believe that this somehow makes you a very special person.

What is it that makes you special? Perhaps you cannot verbalize it. The stories, the old stories that are told and retold, somehow make you a part of something bigger, grander, more important than the harsh reality of your life as Pharaoh's slave.

According to these stories, there was a man who lived even farther back than the time of Israel. His name was Abraham. It was said

9

of him that he was the special friend of the gods—or was it that he was a friend of the *father* of the gods, the *one* god who rules all others?

You cannot imagine how this could be. Is not Pharaoh god? The crocodiles, the bulls, the wind—are they not all gods? How could this Abraham, father of the Israelite clan, have known the *one* god? Such a strange story! And so hard to believe in the face of all that you see and learn in Egypt.

Your elders fear that the ancient stories will be forgotten. You yourself don't really understand the meaning of the stories, yet you marvel that they are the only thing in all of Egypt which *Apiru* can call their own. Still, you wonder, what can all these stories mean? What difference do they really make?

One day you hear of an incident in a labor camp downriver from your own. An *Apiru* who somehow managed to gain favor with Pharaoh's daughter—one *Mosheh*—strikes and kills an Egyptian. He flees to the desert, east across the Sea of Reeds and into the land of Midian. You think about the incident every now and then, but soon forget all about it.

One day, some years later, *Mosheh* returns from the desert. He is not the same man who fled from Egypt years before. He has aged, yes, but changed also in a way that is difficult to describe. He tells an amazing, nearly incredible story. He is sent, he says, to bring the Israelites out of Egypt. When you ask him by whom he is sent, he replies that he is sent by God. "But what is this god's name?" you ask. *Mosheh* replies, *"Ehyeh asher ehyeh*. I AM WHO I AM is his name. I AM has sent me. He is the God of Israel and the God of Abraham, and he has instructed me to lead you out of Egypt and into your *own* land, a land that God himself will give you, a land flowing with milk and honey."*

If you can imagine yourself living through the scene just described, then you are in a proper frame of mind to begin reading the Old Testament. In order to understand these books which we collectively call the Old Testament, you must be able to think and feel at least a little bit like an ancient Israelite who lived through the events recorded in the Old Testament. You must become part Hebrew—at least mentally—in order to understand the Old Testament.

The world of the Hebrew people at the time of Moses was

---

*In a number of instances through this book I will use imaginary conversations and/or paraphrases of Scripture to assist our understanding of a particular period of Israel's story. Where an exact quote is used a scriptural citation will be supplied.

radically different from the world of the 20th century. To project *our* thoughts, *our* values, *our* beliefs back into that time would be seriously to distort the message of the Old Testament. What we must do is to read the Old Testament on *its* terms and not on our own. We must suspend our preconceived notions of God, religion, morality, justice, time and "scientific" truth. We must drop this and a lot of the other 20th-century baggage that we carry around with us when we approach the Old Testament. We must let the people of the Old Testament simply be themselves.

Before we take up the actual story of the people, let's first establish what our method of analyzing the Book of Exodus (Ex) and the other Old Testament books will be. Let us say a word about how best to approach the written record we will be studying.

AVOIDING FUNDAMENTALISM

There are two levels of inquiry to be considered as we begin our journey through Exodus and through the rest of the Old Testament:

1) *Face-Value Level.* The first level of inquiry deals with the literal narrative itself as it has come down to us. We will call this level the *face-value* level. It concerns itself with the words of Scripture, the basic story of people, God and events. For example, in Ex 14, simply considering the words on the face-value level, we read that the Egyptians chased the Israelites to the Sea of Reeds (called the "Red Sea" in some translations). There Yahweh worked a great miracle. He led the Israelites through the waters unharmed but brought the Egyptians to destruction. On the face-value level, therefore, we see pursuit by enemies, Yahweh's miracle and the subsequent escape.

2) *Meaning Level.* The second level of inquiry into Scripture deals with the *significance* of the words. We will call this the *meaning* level. It concerns itself with the intent and purpose of the persons who wrote the words—their values, judgments and viewpoints. For example, in the scene just described, was the writer simply trying to record an event, or was he also teaching something to his readers about the way Yahweh wanted to relate to his people? As we shall see shortly, the writer wanted to do much more than simply leave behind a chronicle of events. He was trying to promote his own viewpoint about what the escape through the sea *meant*.

To understand Exodus and the Old Testament properly, we must approach the text of Scripture on both its face-value level and its meaning level. Often the two levels coincide, but many times they do not. Often the writer means much more by the words than is evident from a cursory reading of the text.

Some students of Scripture make no distinction between the face-value level and the meaning level. They assume that the full meaning of the text is revealed explicitly and solely in the words themselves. In the example given above, they would see the author of the event as simply a passive observer who wrote down what he saw without any desire to inject his own perspective into the narrative. This school of thought is known as *fundamentalism*.

It is very difficult to defend this approach to Scripture since there are often inconsistencies—even contradictions—in the *words* of Scripture. When we come across such inconsistencies or contradictions, we have three choices: (1) We can say, as the fundamentalists do, "It's all a mystery and we just have to believe." (2) We can say, as do many well-educated non-believers, "The Bible is simply a work of religious literature, no different from any other ancient book." (3) We can take the position embodied in this book—to search out how and why inconsistencies appear, their purpose and what they reveal both about the persons who wrote the words and the audience for whom the words were intended. In short, we can search for the true *meaning* of the words. This search leads us to the story *behind* the Old Testament. It is this story that ultimately makes the history of salvation relevant to us today.

Before looking at the whole sweep of Exodus, let us take just two examples to see how this two-level approach works in practice. Turn first to Ex 9:6. There we read that the fifth plague which Yahweh sent on the Egyptians destroyed *all* the Egyptian livestock. Yet just four verses later in 9:10 we find that the sixth plague—the outbreak of boils—infested man and *beast*. If all of the livestock had already been destroyed, how could the beasts have later been inflicted with boils? That question, you see, reveals our 20th-century logical mind at work. The author of this scene wasn't burdened by our philosophical mind-set. He wasn't trying to write a journalistic description of events. He was concerned with *teaching* a particular point to his readers: that Yahweh was greater and more powerful than the bogus gods of Egypt and that the Israelites in relying on Yahweh would have dominance over their enemies.

Turn next to Ex 14:15-31, the crossing of the Sea of Reeds. Here we find differing descriptions of the same event written by *different* authors. For example, in 14:16 we read that Moses' stretching forth his staff was the cause of the parting of the sea. In 14:21 we find instead that *Yahweh* drove back the sea with a strong easterly wind, making the sea into dry land. Yet in 14:22 the windswept landscape is abruptly forgotten and the Israelites are now walking between walls of water. In 14:24-25, Yahweh's fierce glance is said to have been the cause of the Egyptians' downfall, while in 14:26-28 it is Moses' outstretched hand which causes the walls of water to tumble down upon the pursuing soldiers and saves the day for the Israelites.

What do we do in the face of these differing descriptions? Do we cry "Heresy!" because someone dares to suggest there are discrepancies in God's Holy Word? Do we say, "See, the Bible is merely humanly inspired literature," as do many proponents of 20th-century analytical rationalism? Or do we take that third approach, neither denying the evidence provided by the text, nor betraying our faith in the underlying truth of Scripture? Let us explore where that third alternative leads.

A BETTER APPROACH

By taking this alternative we are able to avail ourselves of a rich treasury of knowledge gleaned for us over many years of study by patient, dedicated and, unfortunately, sometimes maligned individuals called Scripture scholars. These men (and, more recently, women) have delved into Scripture and arrived at generally held conclusions about the broad purpose, scope and meaning of the text. As in any field of study, there are differences among biblical scholars on many fine points. In this book I will focus on the broad areas of agreement rather than technicalities which may be disputed, and I will summarize widely held conclusions without explaining how they were reached.

The scholars' conclusion is that there were several authors at work in the Book of Exodus (as well as in the other four books of the *Pentateuch*, the name given to the five-book unit comprised of Genesis, Exodus, Leviticus, Numbers and Deuteronomy). Since we don't know the authors' real names, they have been given nicknames and abbreviations, according to their area of interest and their perspective in writing:

1) J, for *Yahwist*, whose name for God was *Jahweh* or, as we spell it in English, *Yahweh;*
2) E, for *Elohist*, whose name for God was *El*, singular, and *Elohim*, plural (which in ancient Hebrew frequently was used in the same sense as the singular, *El*);
3) P, for *Priestly*, whose interest was to promote the liturgy, cult, worship and rituals of the Jewish religion as they were developed much later in our story, and certainly much later than the time of the Exodus from Egypt;

13

4) D, for *Deuteronomist*, whose writing developed later than that of either J or E, but before P's. D's attention centered on calling the Israelites of his age (centuries after the Exodus event) to return to a strict observance of the laws given by God to Moses on Mt. Sinai.

In later chapters of this book we will discuss in greater detail the interests and backgrounds of J, E, P and D. For the moment, let us just remember that there *are* different sources to consider as we probe into the pages of Exodus.

Now let us apply what we have just said about these different sources to our discussion of Ex 14 above. In 14:16 the role of Moses appears uppermost. Here P is at work emphasizing the importance of the man Moses in the events. The angel of God mentioned in 14:19 comes from E, who frequently used "angel of God" to mean God himself. The emphasis on Yahweh's use of the east wind in 14:21b was a means J used to highlight the importance of Yahweh's *direct intervention* on behalf of the Israelites. (D didn't make a contribution to this particular scene.)

The question one might ask at this point is, "Which is the older, or the more correct, or the more original source?" The answer is "all of the above." Neither J, E or P, in the example that we cited above, "made up their story." Each account tells the truth, and each account relies on the original core of the story as it was transmitted by a long line of *narrators*.

Remember that the first of these *narrators* lived long before J, E, P or D lived and *wrote*. These narrators were such people as the old, bearded wise man from the scene we imagined at the beginning of this chapter, who passed on the story of the patriarchs which we read today in Genesis. Stories about the Exodus from Egypt would have been passed on in the same fashion. When the eventual authors wrote down their version of this oral tale, each had access to the core story itself, yet each wrote it down according to his own perspective.

PUTTING THE PICTURE TOGETHER

The story of how we got *our* story of the Exodus event—in a nutshell—goes something like this. J dates from about the time of King David's court, some 250 years after the Exodus. E was started about a hundred years later than J in the separated northern kingdom. (see Chapter Seven). D was begun not long before 622 B.C., drawing on many of the same traditions available to E in the northern part of the divided realm (see Chapter Seven). P, finally, was the "editor-in-chief," putting the finishing touches on J, E and D and adding his own account of the story beginning around the year 500 B.C.

So we see that while the Book of Exodus concerns itself with events occurring about 1250 B.C., the final written description of those events dates from around 500 B.C. and even later.

During the intervening 700 years a lot happened! Much of what happened obviously colored the perspective of later editors. If we were to write a history of the Middle Ages today, we could not help but be affected by all that we know concerning our own age as we wrote about people living in the 1300's. The sixth-century B.C. editors of Exodus were no different in this respect. Nevertheless, one point must be stressed: Each editor who had a hand in writing Exodus relied scrupulously on the *core story* as it was transmitted to him. When we read the writings of these later editors, therefore, we are reading about events which, in some form, actually happened.

We have no more reason to doubt the integrity and veracity of these editors than we have for doubting the words of other ancient historians, such as Herodotus, Thucidydes or Polybius. If there was a Pericles, then there was a Moses. If there was a Peloponnesian War, then there was an Israelite escape from Egypt. If there was a founding of ancient Rome, there was the formation of an Israelite nation at Mt. Sinai which based its life on the covenant given to Moses.

It is the story of the beginnings of this nation Israel which is recorded for us in Exodus. The outline of the book is rather simple:

1) Ex 1—15:21. *The deliverance from Egypt*—how Yahweh through Moses led a band of religiously ignorant Hebrew slaves out of Egypt and into the desert.

2) Ex 15:22—18. *The people's early life in the desert*—how they often grumbled and complained and wished aloud they had stayed in Egypt.

3) Ex 19—24. *Yahweh's making of the covenant with Israel*—and his establishment of the Ten Commandments and lesser laws.

4) Ex 25—31. *Ritual details*—lengthy, tedious and often confusing passages devoted to Yahweh's instructions to construct the desert sanctuary, Ark of the Covenant and other sacred articles and instruments which were to be used by the people in their worship.

5) Ex 32—34. *The Israelites' first act of apostasy*—of which there would be many more—and the subsequent reestablishment of the law code and covenant.

6) Ex 35—40. *More ritual details*—an almost exact duplication

of Ex 25—31, illustrating how the commands given by
Yahweh in those chapters were put into effect.

THE ESSENTIAL TEACHINGS OF EXODUS

Since excellent Biblical commentaries abound, it is not my
purpose to present a detailed analysis of the various sections of Exodus
outlined above. Instead, I will simply highlight its essential teachings in
terms of what I call three "revolutions" in religion that emerge from the
time of the Exodus event: (1) a revolution in *understanding the nature
of God;* (2) a revolution in *human relationship with God;* and (3) a
revolution in *people's relationships with each other.*

Three deep impressions had been etched into the human psyche
by the time Moses came down from Mt. Sinai, his face aglow like the
noonday sun. Three currents of divine energy had been set free to flow
out into the desert, nourishing the Israelites as they began an ordeal of
purgation that was to last 40 years and prepare them to enter the
Promised Land.

First Revolution: A God Who Controls Time

The first revolution involves a whole new way of thinking about
God. Consider what Yahweh did for a moment. He intervened in
human history to perform an act utterly unlike anything done before by
any god theretofore known to humanity. Other gods—like those who
worshiped them—were bound by a powerful and mysterious entity, the
entity of *time.* Their existence was tied to the seasons of the year and
the other endless cycles of nature. Human beings could not control their
gods but, it was hoped, they could appease and manipulate them by
offering sacrifices, which supposedly prompted the gods to take some
control over time and nature.

Nevertheless, time always seemed to be greater than the gods.
The great myths of the pagans always depicted the gods as subservient
to the rhythms and cycles of nature, as were human beings. Time was
the great force. Yet it had no purpose, no destiny, no end. Things
would continue forever as they had before.

Then, suddenly, a deeply startling event occurs. A God appears
to Moses proclaiming that his name is of an entirely different order than
names held by other gods. His name, he says, is simply *I AM.* Unlike
the other gods, I AM (or Yahweh*) daringly and dramatically

---

*The word *Yahweh* stems from the Hebrew verb "to be," and has become the
English pronunciation for expressing the name which God gave to Moses.

proclaims, in effect, "There is nothing—no force, no aspect of nature, no god that can control or dominate me. Those other gods must have particular names, whether of animals, the sun, the moon or Pharaoh, because they are limited and bound by a certain inherent quality which defines them. *I*, on the other hand, *AM*!"

Here was a revolutionary happening—a God appearing who was outside of time and nature, and unaffected by them. To drive home the point, *I AM* intervened in a specific, definite, unrepeatable moment of time—the crossing of the Sea of Reeds—and said by his actions, "I will control and dominate this particular moment of time. I am greater than time. It cannot resist my action to affect and mold it. I choose to enter into time at this point, to lead this people Israel through the sea to safety. *I AM* will do this."

And Yahweh did do it, to the amazement of the Israelites, who remember to this day that moment when Yahweh bore them "on eagles' wings" to himself (Ex 19:4). This moment was the true beginning of the Israelites' life as a people.

To commemorate the beginning of their new life with Yahweh, the Israelites instituted the feast of Passover. "This day is to be a day of remembrance for you," P writes in Ex 12:14, "and you must celebrate it as a feast in Yahweh's honor." It was typical of the Israelites to solemnize a great event in their history by ritualizing that event, thus preserving the past into the present. When Jews celebrate Passover to this day, they participate *now* in the Exodus event that took place *then*, just as Christians who participate in the Eucharistic celebration believe that the Jesus of the Last Supper is fully present *now* in the breaking of the bread. This ancient understanding of the deeper dimensions of time is alien to many people in our day. Yet the Exodus event reveals to us precisely this deeper, fuller significance of time.

With the entrance of Yahweh into history, religious time began. Time now had a purpose, a meaning and a destiny. No longer did humankind have only endless cycles to look forward to: Now began the possibility of a conclusion to time—a final moment when reality as it had hitherto been experienced would change into something radically different. None of this, of course, was in the minds of the Israelites at the moment of the Exodus. Probably their only concern was escaping Pharaoh's clutches. We, however, who study the event in its three-millennium context, are able to understand the deeper significance of what happened that day at the Sea of Reeds.

Second Revolution: Yahweh, God of the Covenant
The next momentous occurrence in the story of Yahweh and the

Israelites takes place far out into the desert, at a mountain which J calls Mt. Sinai (E calls the same location Mt. Horeb). An understanding of this next event is absolutely essential to a further understanding of the Bible. In this scene (Ex. 19—24), Yahweh and Israel enter into a covenant.

What is a covenant? A covenant is basically a promise which leads to a binding obligation between two or more *covenantors,* or parties to the covenant. In today's legal parlance we still call the parties to a contract "covenantors."

If we look closely at the Book of Exodus we find that two types of covenants—one conditional and one unconditional—are described. In 19:5 Yahweh says, "If you obey my voice...you of all the nations shall be my very own...." In other words, Yahweh makes a conditional promise, requiring a promise of acceptance in return. This the people give in 19:8: "All that Yahweh has said, we will do."

This understanding of the covenant—which comes most likely from D, and perhaps also from J and E—has a strong element of mutuality contained in it. "*If* this, *then* that " which implies "*if not* this, *then not* that." In other words, according to this view of the covenant, if the people backed out of the deal and disobeyed Yahweh, he was no longer obligated to regard them as his people.

Another view, that of an *unconditional* covenant, was held by P, the "editor-in-chief" of Exodus. Since he inserted Ex 19 into his final product, he obviously felt that "conditional covenant" was one valid understanding. But P wanted also to include another viewpoint.

By the time P made his contribution to Exodus he had already recorded two examples of unconditional covenants in the Book of Genesis (Gn 9:8 and 17:7). P wanted to link up the Sinai Covenant with these earlier examples of unconditional covenants. We see examples of P's attempt to do this in Ex 6:2-8, where Yahweh unconditionally promises Moses (6:7) to adopt the Israelites "as my own people." Yahweh's intentions concerning this unconditional covenant are revealed earlier by P in Ex 2:24, where Yahweh is said to have "called to mind his [unconditional] covenant with Abraham, Isaac and Jacob."

Thus we have in Exodus two differing understandings of the covenant. It will be essential to keep these two understandings in mind as we proceed.

Despite these divergent opinions about the nature of the covenant, one thing was clear by the conclusion of the Sinai event: A new people had been formed by Yahweh according to rational legal principle. Yahweh was not going to act in a haphazard, unpredictable fashion, as did the gods of the pagans. He was going to establish for his people the precise structure and elements of the relationship into which they were entering.

This in itself was a major revolution in religious history. God limiting his prerogatives by an agreement with human beings? Unheard of! Yet that is precisely what Exodus tells us Yahweh did—all freely, unprompted, completely on his own initiative, without any prior meritorious conduct on the part of the Israelites.

Third Revolution: Yahweh's People

Not only does Exodus overturn the way people looked at their relationship with God; it also offers a revolutionary way for a people to relate to each other. Even though Yahweh worked through a mediator, Moses, in making the covenant with Israel, *each* Israelite was considered a co-covenantor *directly* with Yahweh. The humblest goatherd, in Yahweh's eyes, was of equal value with Moses.

Such a view of society was unthinkable in the pagan countries where pharaohs, kings and satraps lorded it over their human property, and even declared themselves to be gods.

These three revolutionary concepts in religion set the stage for a journey in faith that was to be unique among the peoples of the ancient Near East. But though that journey began with a "mountaintop" experience, it was soon to lead into the desert and beyond where the people would be challenged to make their response to Yahweh in the concrete and practical realities of everyday life.

CHAPTER TWO

'THE WATERS OF MERIBAH'

Numbers

'**O**kay, Moses, what do we do now?" That might have been a question you or I would have asked had we lived in the desert with the Israelites who escaped from Egypt. The excitement was over. The "big event" had been concluded. Yahweh's power had been demonstrated at the Sea of Reeds and the Sinai Covenant had been solemnized. We can imagine how the wonders of the past few months could begin to recede into the background of our awareness and how the practical necessities of surviving in the hot, dry desert would start to assert themselves.

"Were those 'peak moments' of the Exodus and the covenant real?" we might have been tempted to ask. "Or did we just imagine them? And what are we going to do now that we're here? At least in Egypt we had something to do all day long, and plenty of food to eat— especially lots of delicious *meat*! Here in this desert we don't know from one minute to the next whether we'll even have enough water to drink. And Moses—I'm not so sure about him anymore. Why does he get to make all the decisions? Didn't God call *all* of us to be his special people?"

If you can imagine having some of these questions and doubts had you been an Israelite adrift in the barren wasteland of the Negeb some 30 centuries ago, then you are in a good position to approach the Book of Numbers (Nm).

This book records the second stage in the formation of the Israelite people. The first stage had been all Yahweh's doing. Now it was time for the people to demonstrate their response to Yahweh's call to become a holy people, a consecrated nation. What would that response be? Let us turn to the pages of Numbers to find our answer.

If you are approaching Numbers for the first time you may become confused. The material seems to be presented in a hodgepodge, disorganized fashion. First of all, in Nm 1—4, we read about the census of the people and notice that much is said about the tribe of Levi. Then, in Nm 5—8, we find some peculiar laws and more about the Levites. When we get to Nm 9, we may think we've finally gotten to the interesting part. But not long after (Nm 15—19), we digress into such unstimulating subjects as the color of the cord to be attached to tassels and the proper disposition of the ashes of red heifers burnt in sacrifice.

The plot seems to pick up a little in Nm 20, and we are even treated to the tale of a talking donkey. To our disappointment, however, the talking donkey story and its sequel only lead us back to a further account of the Levites, another census and more about laws, regulations, rituals and feasts (Nm 26—30). Finally, in Nm 31—36, we accompany the Israelites through a number of successful military skirmishes east of the Jordan. We leave them, at the end of the book, poised to cross the Jordan and ready to invade Canaan.

What coherent message, if any, ties these seemingly incoherent passages of the book together? A good way to begin our analysis is to read the "action chapters" first, and then come back to read the chapters on law and ritual later. Therefore, let us postpone for a moment any discussion of Nm 1—8, 15—19 and 26—30.

THE 'ACTION CHAPTERS' OF NUMBERS

In Nm 9 we find the Israelites ready to depart from the foot of Mt. Sinai for the Promised Land. We see that they didn't get far before they started doubting and complaining. "Who will give us meat to eat?" they asked. "Think of the fish we used to eat free in Egypt, the cucumbers, melons, leeks, onions and garlic! Here we are wasting away, stripped of everything; there is nothing but manna for us to look at!" (11:4-6).

Moses grew understandably upset with all this griping. Here he was trying to lead the people to the Promised Land, and they couldn't get their thoughts off suppertime. "Where is your faith?" he must have been tempted to shout at them. "Didn't you see what Yahweh did for us at the Sea of Reeds? Are your memories so short?" This first major griping episode ended with Yahweh providing so many quail for the people to eat that the birds were stacked up three feet deep in the Israelite camp.

Yahweh also intervened by giving Moses a body of elders who would help him shoulder the responsibilities of leadership. When Moses had called 70 of the leading men together, Yahweh "took some of the spirit that was on him [Moses] and put it on the seventy elders" (11:25). In other words, the authors (J and E at this point) are telling us that Yahweh gave the 70 some portion of the divine wisdom which he had previously reserved only for Moses. The 70, therefore, would now validly share Moses' authority. (We see here the formation of the institution of "judges," the charismatic leaders handpicked by Yahweh to lead his people. We will take up the full story of the judges in Chapter Four.)

The turning point of Numbers occurs in Nm 13. Moses commissions spies to reconnoiter the Canaanite territory. Twelve men are sent; 12 men see the same countryside, the same people, the same fortified cities, the same towns. Ten spies return and give this report: "The country we went to reconnoiter is a country that devours its inhabitants. Every man we saw there was of enormous size" (13:32). But two spies, Caleb and Joshua, present a different version of the encounter with the land and its people: "We must march in…and conquer this land: we are well able to do it" (13:31). Which report do you think the people accepted? The negative one, of course! As an old Hebrew proverb says, "We do not see things as *they* are, but as *we* are." The author of that proverb could have had no better historical episode from which to draw his conclusion.

Here was the Israelites' golden opportunity. "All right, folks," Yahweh seemed to be saying. "You saw what I did at the Sea of Reeds. You've seen how I've fed you in this desert, first with manna and now with quail. So get ready to enter your new homeland. I'll march ahead of you to clear a path. Don't worry about a thing."

It didn't work. The people could not seize the moment. They were ensnared once again by their fears and their doubts. Moses, Aaron, Joshua and Caleb must have turned almost livid with anger: "What! That land is ours for the taking! Will you *ever* stop doubting Yahweh's word?" (See Nm 14:9-10.) They almost got stoned for their trouble.

Fortunately, Yahweh intervened again and said, in effect, "I can see that you people just aren't ready for the gift I wanted to give you. You need a little more preparation—a little more desert—before you are mature enough to enter your homeland. Very well, then, you'll have to spend 40 years in this wasteland—one year for every day the spies spent in Canaan—and then maybe you will believe my words."

The Israelites had been given their opportunity for a new life, but did not recognize it. They chose fear rather than faith and condemned themselves to a longer period of hardship, suffering and homelessness.

DAILY LIFE IN THE DESERT

What does one do all day long in the desert, anyway? Specifically, what did the Israelites do for the 40 years *they* spent there? No one knows every detail, of course, but one answer can be found in the chapters we omitted from the discussion above, chapters which concern themselves with law and ritual (1—8, 15—19 and 26—30).

The author of those chapters is the overall editor of Numbers, our now-familiar source, P. P presents the people as principally a *worshiping* people. What they did all day, when they weren't out fighting their enemies, was to attend to the details of religious practice.

In order to understand why P is so fascinated with laws, rituals, sacrifices, the priesthood and the Levites, we need to look ahead about seven centuries to the time P and his school lived and wrote. We'll do this in greater detail later (see pp. 109-113).

For right now, let us simply say that P's literary concerns centered around law and ritual, cult and priesthood because that was the core of Jewish life *at the time P lived*.

Notice that I said *Jewish* life. There were no *Jews* in the desert with Moses. At least, they weren't called that then. The ancestors of the Jews—our wandering Israelites—had an understanding of religion that was much less complex than that of P and his fellow Jews who lived at the time of the Exile and after. For reasons which we shall discuss in later chapters, Jewish religion by P's time had become almost entirely ritualistic and liturgical.

Therefore, in order to *authenticate* the new Jewish religion, P wrote his contemporary practices back into history, associating them with Moses, Aaron and the first days of the Israelite desert community. He wanted his contemporaries to see that what he and the other priests of his own era taught had Moses' stamp of approval. He thus presented contemporary religious practices as if they actually were going on right from the start of the Israelite experience.

A little common sense, as well as the study of archaeology and history, will substantiate that this is what P was doing. The P chapters in Numbers depict a community with a highly developed, well-organized religious structure. Such a structure was hardly suitable for

24

nomads wandering about in the desert. For example, how did Israelites constantly on the move manage to develop the crafts and skills (to say nothing of the raw materials) needed to make the many brass and metal implements described by P as essential to normative religious life? How, to be more precise, did they come up with the 250 metal incense burners described in Nm 16? We know that when the Israelites actually entered Canaan their main enemies, the Philistines, were able to dominate the Israelites for so long precisely because the Israelites were so unfamiliar with metalworking.

The entire description of these P chapters applies to a sedentary, stable community which had already experienced a long tradition of sophisticated religious practice. P's description of religious life certainly does not apply to the loose aggregation of nomads which Moses had difficulty keeping in line in the Negeb.

Does this mean that P was an absolute fabricator, promoting his own narrow interests by deceitfully rewriting history? Not at all. We have to get over our 20th-century hang-up about "facts" if we are to understand P's approach.

To P and the Jews of his time, the central "fact" was that the Israelites had been called by Yahweh to be a *priestly* people, a people set apart for worship. The entire nation was thus to be a *holy* people, a witness to the Gentiles of the holiness and majesty of Yahweh. That was *the* fact, and to deny this would be to deny a fundamental truth found in Scripture.

A subsidiary fact on which P relied was contained in the oral and written record of Israelite desert life: *From their earliest days* the Israelites *had* given a prominent place to worship, even in those confused and disorganized years in the desert. They had, in fact, tried to be precisely a holy, worshiping community of believers. They failed repeatedly to do this, but never failed to look upon holiness and worship as the *constituent elements* of their life as a people, right from the start of their existence.

P was, therefore, by no means fabricating the Israelite emphasis on worship. He was merely dressing up this aspect of early Israelite life in contemporary clothing so that his fellow Jews would recognize it more readily. In doing this he unashamedly promoted priestly doctrine, but he did not "make up" the fact of the early Israelite emphasis on worship.

P's basic teaching in Numbers is that the priests comprised an elite body in Israelite life, separate and distinct from the laity. Priests were the principal intermediaries between people and God. The Levites were lesser functionaries who assisted the priests and carried out the more mundane chores necessary to the running of a temple cult.

From this basic hierarchical foundation stemmed much else relating to Jewish religious life—laws relating to ritual and worship, tithing, sacrifice, the sabbath, feasts and celebrations. We get a brief overview of these aspects of Jewish religious life in P's chapters in Numbers. If you find *these* chapters tedious and uninteresting, wait until you get to Leviticus! (See Chapter Eleven.) There we shall read P in all his ponderous glory as he sets forth the complete charter of the Jewish cult.

Now, let us turn from P for a moment and go back again to the J and E narrative we were considering earlier.

More Action: On to the Promised Land

In Nm 20 we find that the community was engaged once again in its favorite activity—complaining, this time about lack of water. Moses had just about reached the limit of his tolerance. When Yahweh told him to command a rock to give forth water, Moses decided first to deliver a sermon to the people. "Listen now, you rebels. Shall we make water gush from this rock for you?" (Nm 20:10). In other words, Moses says, "Look at me, you bunch of doubters! See how faithless you are! I'm going to make water come right out of this rock."

Well, water did come out of the rock, but Moses went a little too far to suit Yahweh in the direction of condemning the people. All Yahweh wanted was for his people to have water; he didn't want them to be condemned in the process. Moses, therefore, was punished.

"I'll be the one who decides when and how to teach my people a lesson," Yahweh seems to tell Moses in 20:12. He says in effect, "You just follow orders. Because you didn't do this strictly, I'm not going to let you lead the people into the Promised Land."

This seems to us a very harsh penalty for such a faithful and loyal servant. But, as we shall continually discover in the Old Testament, "Yahweh's ways are not our ways" (see Is 55:8). Yahweh's principal concern, we find, is to teach his people how to be holy—that is, how to be more like Yahweh himself. This often means, as we have just seen in this incident with Moses, that Yahweh will take a course of action that appears to us to be harsh and unfair.

Events proceed swiftly from this point on. J and E assume the passage of time, skipping over the 40-year stay at Kadesh that seems to have begun with the incidents in Nm 13—14 and conclude with those in Nm 20. The speed and pace of the military drive during the last few months of the Israelites' desert sojourn set the theme for J and E: God's people proceed to the Promised Land in triumph over the enemies they meet along the way.

The Israelite army, apparently organized and trained for combat during the desert years, is now a formidable fighting force. It moves into the region opposite Palestine, east of the Jordan. The Israelites defeat two petty kings and are ready to attack the land of Moab—the last unconquered territory lying east of the Jordan. If Moab falls, the Promised Land itself is next.

Balak, king of Moab, realized he was in trouble: "Look how this people coming from Egypt has overrun the whole countryside; they have settled at my door" (22:5). Balak sends for one Balaam, a prophet of some renown, and beseeches him to utter a few curses and threats over the advancing army. But God visits the prophet by night and warns him against cursing the people. He may respond to the king's invitation but must say only what God directs.

The story contains a delightful J anecdote (22:22-35) which takes place as Balaam is astride his donkey on the way to see the king. The *donkey* perceives the presence of the angel of Yahweh on the trail and stubbornly refuses to challenge the vision. Balaam beats the innocent beast until the donkey, suddenly gifted with speech, explains to the suitably humbled prophet what is happening! Again, the prophet is directed to deliver *God's* message rather than a "curse-on-demand."

Balaam finally reaches the king and, much to Balak's displeasure, Balaam not only does not curse the Israelites, he instead bursts forth into praise and blessing of them. He prophesies that the Israelites will become as numerous as the specks of dust in a dust cloud. The J-E account ends abruptly with the conclusion of Balaam's prophecy (24:25).

After a five-chapter digression, P picks up the narrative again in Nm 31. The Israelites are on the move once more, slaughtering their enemies. Curiously, they kill Balaam himself during this military campaign (31:8). In the final chapters of Numbers, the booty seized in battle is distributed, the lands soon to be conquered in Palestine are allocated in advance among the tribes and Moses' successor, Joshua, makes ready for the final push into Palestine.

THE MESSAGE OF NUMBERS

What then is the message of the Book of Numbers for us? It is this: We are the Israelites who have escaped from Egypt. We have been delivered by God from our prior state of ignorance, sin and misery, and we are on our way to the Promised Land. We are presented, like the

Israelites, with a golden opportunity to move in and capture this land—it is ours for the asking. A life of joy, happiness, fellowship and wealth awaits us, if and when we decide we want it.

Which advance report about the land will we accept? The first says, "Let's go back to Egypt; at least we knew what we had there. What we saw in the new land terrified us! Freedom and peace and happiness are too unfamiliar to us. Surely we weren't meant to possess them."

The second report is completely at odds with the first. It says, "We were created for happiness, not misery, and we will only find such happiness in the Promised Land. What are we waiting for? Let's move in and take it. All it requires is a little faith that God actually wants us to possess the land—and faith as well that he will get us there."

Alas, human history demonstrates we have chosen to accept the first report and to reject the second. We seem to feel ourselves destined for misery. And so we stumble around, lost in our chosen environment of suspicion, doubt, warfare, greed and selfishness.

Yet some of us, like Caleb and Joshua, profit from the desert experience. For these leaders the desert becomes a place of self-denial and total reliance on Yahweh. In the desert, such persons learn to surrender control to Yahweh and to rely on him for the next step in their lives. They are purged of their doubts, fears and compulsions. These leaders call us to advance upon the plains of Moab, to the heights above Jericho where we can see the vast panorama of riches which God has displayed before us.

What is our decision? Do we follow those who call us forward, or do we listen to those urging us to stay behind? The choice is ours. Perhaps we have not yet surrendered control to Yahweh. If so, we may need a little more time in the desert before we can advance into the Promised Land. This is what Yahweh wanted of his people Israel—surrender to him of their self-control and submission to *his* control. How thoroughly had the Israelites opted for this submission to Yahweh when they came down from the cliffs of Moab and marched toward the Jordan? How similar to their choice is our own? Let us join the Israelites as they reach the eastern banks of the Jordan and follow them across. By doing this we will find our answers.

CHAPTER THREE

'COME UP FROM THE JORDAN!'

Joshua

'**J**oshua fit the battle of Jericho, and the walls came a-tumblin' down!" That's what the words of an old Negro spiritual have to say about one of the central events in the Book of Joshua (Jos). The Bible's rendition of the same event (Jos 6) is a little more complicated. In fact, the whole book—when closely analyzed—is a good deal more complicated than one would think after a light reading of its 24 chapters.

On the surface the chronology of events related in Joshua is as follows:

1) a swift conquest of the Promised Land (1—12);
2) a perfunctory apportionment of the now-conquered pagan territories (13—19);
3) the resolution of miscellaneous details about the Levites and the tribes who would remain east of the Jordan (20—22);
4) Joshua's farewell speech, followed by a covenant ratification ceremony at Shechem (23—24).

This neat, well-packaged description leaves one thinking, "That surely was easy! The Israelites marched right in, conquered the new land as Yahweh had promised they would, and then settled down to a happy, peaceful existence." This highly stylized account of the actual happenings was designed by the editor of Joshua to leave us with *just* such an impression.

To understand what I mean by that remark, we must consider once again the question of the interplay between the face-value level and the meaning level of biblical interpretation (see p. 11). Perhaps in no other book of the Bible is the dissonance between these two levels as striking as in Joshua.

First, much of what is related in Joshua is at variance with other biblical accounts of the same events (such as those given in the Book of Judges, for example) and in conflict as well with the findings of literary, historical and archaeological research. For example, the evidence indicates that both Jericho and Ai, two cities stated in Joshua to have been destroyed by the Israelites, were actually uninhabited rubble heaps by the time of the Israelite "invasion." How is it, then, that the Israelites "conquered" the cities?

Second, the "invasion" described in Joshua would lead one to believe that all 12 tribes acted together in *blitzkrieg* fashion and easily subdued the land. In Judges, however, we find that the "invasion" was more like a gradual encroachment by *some* tribes into Canaanite areas and that the Israelite "victory" was hardly decisive. What's more, the newly settling tribes lived in almost constant peril of being uprooted and dispossessed by the pagans.

Since it thus appears that Joshua was not intended to be scientific history, what *was* it intended to be? What deeper purpose underlies the narrative of events? Why is there a difference in Joshua between the face-value level and meaning level of the text? To answer these questions, we must get to know a little bit about our authors.

THE DIFFERENT TRADITIONS IN JOSHUA

Since I said *authors*, you may be thinking that we are concerned here with our friends J, E, P and D. Actually J and E don't have anything to do with Joshua. P makes a slight contribution, but it is D who makes the greatest contribution. In addition to P and D, scholars think there are two other writers who contributed to Joshua. These latter two are of lesser significance; thus no one has bothered to give them initials! I will call one *G*, for Gilgal, the shrine where he likely wrote his account, and the other *B*, short for "boundary-setter," which indicates what his principal contribution to the narrative was.

The generally accepted theory about how G, B, P and D all collaborated to give us the Book of Joshua goes something like this.

G: A Possible Eyewitness Source

G is the oldest source. G possibly witnessed the Israelites' crossing of the Jordan and entrance into Canaan. As G remembered things, the man Joshua was the prime mover of events, and the former desert tribes jointly accepted Joshua as their new Moses. G's contribution to Joshua is the core narrative found in Jos 2—9, which describes who did what, when. G is also greatly interested in explaining how various places in the Promised Land received their names (for example, see 7:26).

B: A Real Estate Record

B wrote somewhat later than G. His purpose was to establish the validity of Israelite claims to land in Canaan. As a result, he wrote a real estate record minutely describing the boundaries of land apportioned to the various tribes. B's account is found in Jos 13—19.

P: More Cult and Ritual

P, interested as usual in matters concerning ritual, worship and cult, contributed the story in Jos 22 about the "rival altar" built by the tribes living in the East Jordan area. He contributed a few other miscellaneous notes as well.

D: A Major School of Old Testament Theology

What about D? D was not a single writer, but a particular school of writers who compiled a general history from the Book of Joshua through the Second Book of Kings—a period of roughly six centuries. In addition to those two books, five others bear the imprint of D's writing: Judges, 1 and 2 Samuel, 1 Kings and Deuteronomy. The D tradition was committed to writing beginning in the mid-600's B.C., and the last D editor wrote in the mid-500's B.C. Since so much of the Old Testament was shaped by D, we will now spend some time getting to know this tradition.

BEGINNINGS OF DEUTERONOMIC HISTORY

D's primary theological interest was to stress the conditional nature of the Sinai Covenant (see pp. 17-19). D was the proponent of the "great *if*": "*If* you obey Yahweh's commands, then you will prosper; *if* you don't, then you will succumb to your enemies." The final D editor, who was writing nearly seven centuries after the time of Joshua, wanted to set the stage for the reader of the Joshua/Kings history which was the concern of the D tradition. D wanted to establish from the beginning that the reason for Israel's success was fidelity to Yahweh's covenant; the reason for failure, infidelity.

Thus, right from the start of the Joshua/Kings saga, D sets out to establish the "iffiness" of the Israelites' relationship with Yahweh.

The two central D chapters in Joshua (1 and 23) are filled with this message. For example:

> "But *if* you prove faithless, *if* you make friends with the remnant of those peoples who are still left beside you, *if* you form kinships with them and intermarry, *then* know for certain that Yahweh your God will no longer drive these peoples before you; instead, they will be a snare and a pitfall for you, a scourge to your sides and thorns in your eyes, till you vanish from this good land which Yahweh your God has given you."
>
> (Jos 23:12-13, emphasis added)

Of course, the final D editor, writing in the mid-500's B.C., had just lived through the period when the Israelites had in fact "vanished from the land" (see pp. 78-82). He was thus writing his theological perspective back into the Joshua events which had occurred some seven centuries before his time. He did this in order to show the reader *why* the Israelites eventually lost the Promised Land to their enemies.

The purpose of D throughout the Joshua/Kings saga is to teach a *theological* message. The rough historical narrative merely forms a convenient framework around which the real message is woven. Therefore, it didn't make a great deal of difference to D whether the details were straight—whether, for example, it was Jericho, Ai or some other city that the Israelites destroyed in a certain fashion. To accomplish his purpose, D took the older G and B traditions and tailored them to fit his needs, interweaving the D theology "between the lines." As a result, the *history* in Joshua may be a little garbled, but the *theology* is quite clear.

HOW D TEACHES THEOLOGY IN JOSHUA

The D editor has carefully woven basic themes of that school's theology into the colorful scenes of the Book of Joshua. It might be helpful to isolate some of these themes in specific chapters of the book while comparing them with theological statements in the Book of Deuteronomy (Dt). So, with one finger in our Bibles at Deuteronomy and another at Joshua, we'll look at four aspects of D's thinking: (1) the universality of Yahweh's rule, (2) the necessity of separation from the pagan culture, (3) the call to rely strictly on Yahweh's power and guidance, and (4) Yahweh's fidelity to his promises.

Yahweh: God of Heaven and Earth

Turn to the story of Rahab and the spies (Jos 2:8-21). D took this story from the older G tradition and used it to present one of his favorite themes. In 2:11 Rahab says to the spies, "Yahweh your God is God both in heaven above and on earth beneath." Now turn to Deuteronomy, the fullest expression in the Old Testament of D's theology. In Dt 4:39, D writes, "Yahweh is God indeed, in heaven above as on earth beneath, he and no other." We see that D has used the story of the harlot Rahab to teach a core concept of his theology: Yahweh is Lord of the universe.

Israel: A People Set Apart

Now return to Joshua, this time to 6:17-21. There we read Yahweh's instructions about putting Jericho "under the ban." (The "ban" was a primitive practice of declaring persons or objects as dedicated to the deity and then destroying them. The practice comes from an early period of Israel's history and died out as the nation's moral sense matured.) The reason for the institution of the ban appears in Dt 7:6:

> "You are a people consecrated to Yahweh our God; it is you that Yahweh our God has chosen to be his very own people out of all the peoples on the earth." (Dt 7:6)

Thus, D presents the theoretical basis of the ban in Deuteronomy, and then gives an historical application of it in Jos 6. D did this in order to teach his readers that the Israelites had to be a people set apart, undefiled by pagan ways. To achieve this, D sanctioned the rather extreme method of killing all captives taken in battle, lest some Israelites should be tempted to intermarry with those captives and be converted to their pagan ways.

Look at All Yahweh Has Done

A third example of how D historicized his theology occurs in Jos 23. There, Joshua begins his farewell address to his countrymen in these words:

> "...[Y]ou for your part have witnessed all that Yahweh your God has done to all these nations before your eyes; Yahweh your God himself has fought for you." (Jos 23:3)

In a parallel passage, Moses had called the people together in the desert to give *his* farewell address:

> "You have seen all that Yahweh did before your eyes in the land of Egypt, to Pharaoh, to his servants and to his whole land, the great ordeals your

own eyes witnessed, the signs and those great wonders." (Dt 29:2-3)

D is telling us here that Joshua, like his predecessor Moses, emphasized that it was *Yahweh* who had won the people's battles for them. D constantly stresses this message. The people had to understand that it was *Yahweh* who was in control of their destiny, and not they themselves. Whenever they began to rely on their own power, they faltered. If, however, they placed their confidence and trust strictly in Yahweh, they prospered.

Promises Kept

A final theme which D especially emphasized in Joshua was that Yahweh had kept all of the promises which he made to the people in the desert. Here is a capsule summary:

> So it was that Yahweh gave the Israelites all the land he had sworn to give their fathers. They took possession of it and settled there. Yahweh granted them peace on all their frontiers just as he had sworn to their fathers, and of all their enemies not one had managed to stand against them. Yahweh had given all their enemies into their hands. Of all the promises that Yahweh had made to the House of Israel, not one failed; all were fulfilled. (Jos 21:43-45)

This summary, which in effect says, "And they all lived happily ever after," is hardly historically accurate. As we have already noted, the Book of Judges will depict a situation that was nothing like D's idyllic description in Joshua. To explain the discrepancy between the accounts given in Joshua and Judges, let us remember D's motive in editing Joshua. He wanted to establish the central premise of his theology—namely, that conformity to Yahweh's laws and reliance solely on Yahweh's guidance results in peace and prosperity. He thus presents the time of Joshua as a "golden age" in which the Israelites lived by Yahweh's laws, relied strictly on him and consequently received abundant blessings.

Once D establishes this model age, he then proceeds in the rest of the Joshua/Kings saga to describe how the Israelites abandoned their commitment to Yahweh and were eventually destroyed by their enemies. By emphasizing in Joshua Yahweh's fidelity to his promises, D can then conclude that it was not Yahweh who abandoned his people, but the people who abandoned Yahweh. This is in keeping with D's overall purpose in Joshua and Kings, which is to answer the question of why, in an age much closer to D's time, the nation fell to its enemies and the people were carried into exile.

THE ASSEMBLY AT SHECHEM

There is one final matter in Joshua to consider. It concerns Jos 24, which deals with the assembly at Shechem. The subject matter of this chapter (which combines material from an ancient source, assisted by P and D) reveals much about Israelite life at the beginning of the period of the judges. Notice that Shechem appears for the first time in this chapter. In the preceding chapters of Joshua, we found that first Gilgal and then Shiloh were the centers of the Israelite invasion force. Then, suddenly, Shechem appears. What is the significance of this?

We receive a clue by reading Jos 24:14, 18. In 24:14, it appears that Joshua is telling the assembled people *for the first time* about the need to "put away the gods that your ancestors served beyond the River." Why was this necessary? Moses had already taught this to the Israelites in the desert at least 40 years ago. Was Joshua addressing people who had not been in the desert with the other Israelites? Notice that in 24:18 the assembly says, "We, *too*, will serve Yahweh" (emphasis added). "Too" implies here that Joshua's audience is joining the faith of other Israelites who *already believed* in Yahweh.

What is occurring at Shechem is this: A number of Hebrew tribes descended from Abraham whose ancestors had *not* gone down into Egypt are for the first time pledging themselves to keep the Yahweh Covenant, which their "desert relatives" had entered into years before. The biblical, historical and archaeological evidence indicates that not all of the tribes descended from Jacob crossed the Jordan with Joshua and his band of nomadic followers, because not all of them had entered Egypt in the first place.

Thus, when Joshua and the tribes affiliated with him entered the Promised Land, they encountered their long-lost cousins from centuries before! These stay-at-home tribes welcomed the opportunity to join forces with Joshua and their other relatives who were now settling in Canaan and who brought with them the marvelous story of Yahweh's actions at the Sea of Reeds and in the desert. The native tribes were especially impressed by the ideal of social equality which grew out of the Sinai Covenant (see p. 19). They wanted to be freed from the rule of tyrannical Canaanite despots; thus they gladly accepted the radical political, religious and social ideas which Joshua and his comrades imported from the desert.

An important social and political tradition evolved out of the Shechem assembly. According to this tradition, the various tribes were independent, autonomous units of equal stature and rank before

Yahweh, owing no allegiance to any earthly ruler. "It is Yahweh our God we choose to serve," the tribal leaders affirmed at Shechem. "It is his voice that we will obey" (Jos 24:24).

This noble ideal—that the tribes needed no earthly leader and that each tribe was independent of the other—was to be sorely tested during the time of the judges. Shechem represented the happy age of Israel's youth. It was an age in which the tribes considered themselves to be free and autonomous, an age when they remained uncommitted to any interests larger than those of the tribe.

Israel was soon to leave this happy era and pass into a period of sobering growth. Life in the Promised Land posed grave challenges to the chosen life-style of uncommitted tribal autonomy. Israel grew to find that the Promised Land was filled with perils greater than had been imagined—indeed, perils which threatened the people's very existence.

CHAPTER FOUR

DELIVERERS

Judges

'O Baal, lord of the seasons, protector of the harvest, nourish these crops with your sacred gift of rain! O great Ashtarte, receive now the embrace of your heavenly consort, Baal most high. Give life to these vines and these shoots. Bring forth abundant treasures of grapes and wheat for our nourishment. Let Baal be king! Baal is our god!"

This prayer to the Canaanite god of fertility and his divine mistress Ashtarte was perhaps typical of prayers actually offered by devout Canaanites at the start of their spring planting. Imagine for a moment that you are an Israelite youth living in a fertile valley in Palestine. Your grandfather was a nomad, a desert wanderer who had followed Moses from Mt. Sinai to the banks of the Jordan. Your father had fought under Joshua and had received a rich piece of land from his tribal chieftain when the Promised Land was divided. But your father had never learned the art of farming.

"My son," your father says to you on your 13th birthday, "it is time for us to learn the ways of the land. We must put behind us the ways of the desert. No more will we tend flocks, as I and my father did in the days of Moses and Joshua. If we are to succeed in this new land which Yahweh our God has given us, we must take on the ways of the people who have always lived here. We must learn to live from the soil, my son, so that we can bring prosperity and honor to our household."

"But Father," you respond, "where am I to learn the ways of the farmer? How shall I begin?"

"Ah, let us be clever, my son. We will study the ways of our neighbors. We will learn from them what it is that causes the vine and the shoot to blossom. I have watched the Canaanites. I am learning the secrets of the land."

Together you and your father travel around the valley. You observe the Canaanites at work in the field. You start to talk to some of them. You visit their homes. You share a meal. You begin to learn the mysterious secrets of agriculture. One day a Canaanite neighbor tells you that the success of the crops depends upon the favor of the local gods—Baal and his mistress, Ashtarte. If Baal is pleased with your sacrifice to him in the spring, he will have sexual intercourse with Ashtarte and the fruit of their union will be rich crops of grapes and olives, figs and wheat. If Baal is not pleased with your sacrifice, the crops will fail.

Sometimes—your neighbor continues—to urge Baal into action it is necessary to go to the local Baal temple. There priests and their consecrated mistresses engage in sexual intercourse themselves. This stimulates Baal to act. It reminds him of his sacred duty to humankind. It is a great privilege to give your maiden daughter as mistress to the priest; Baal is pleased by this consecration of your virgin daughter to him. Sometimes, when Baal is angry with people, he may remain silent. Then a greater sacrifice is called for to stir him into action—a daughter, or even a son, must be burnt in offering. Baal will listen then. He will embrace Ashtarte and the crops will grow and multiply.

You and your father leave the house of your Canaanite neighbor and walk in silence for some time. Finally you begin to speak:

"Father, are we to do as this man said?"

"I do not know, my son."

You can see that your father is very troubled, uncertain as to what to think.

"Father," you begin again, "what about all those stories you and Grandfather taught me about Yahweh our God? Does Yahweh know about the Baal god? Is Yahweh stronger than he is? Must we worship Baal too, Father?"

"I do not know, my son. We must think about this. We must talk to our brothers. Such a strange story this man has told us! So unlike *our* ways! And yet, if this is what one must do to become a farmer… I do not know. We will think about it. We will talk to our brothers."

NEW LAND, TOUGH CHOICES

We see the choice this Israelite family had to make. What would *we* have done? Would we have accepted our Canaanite neighbor's explanation of how to become a successful farmer and gone over to Baal worship? Or would we have rejected his words, refused to mix our faith in Yahweh with worship of Baal and struggled alone to decipher the mysteries of agriculture? The choice may not have been easy.

Let us not be too harsh, then, on the Israelites newly settled in the land of Canaan who equivocated in their choice between Yahweh and another god. Keep in mind that they didn't really give up their faith in Yahweh. They simply—as we often do today—accommodated their faith to the pressures of the world about them. They were looking at the practicalities of the situation; they had to learn how to survive in their new homeland.

"After all," they said, "if it is Baal who makes farmers successful, what choice do we have? We'll still worship Yahweh, but we'll call on Baal to take care of our crops."

Yet it was this spirit of equivocation, this accommodation of Yahwism to Baalism, this *religious syncretism*, which was to begin the sad history of Israel's fall from grace. Yahweh's chosen people chose another god. This holy people, this priestly people, this people called by Yahweh to be uniquely his own, entered into a love affair with another god. The story of the remainder of the Joshua/Kings Deuteronomic history is essentially the story of Israel's flirtation with pagan gods, the people's consequent distress, their reconciliation with Yahweh, and their relapse time and again into infidelity. We will see in Chapter Seven and Eight the eventual outcome of this seven-century cycle of infidelity, distress, reconciliation and repeated infidelity. For now, we consider the first stages of that cycle as it appears in the Book of Judges (Jgs).

In Jgs 1 we find ourselves in a different world than the one we left behind in Joshua. The Promised Land is not totally dominated by victorious Israelites, after all. Instead many Canaanites are still left unconquered, even after the Israelite invasion ends.

The Book of Judges is the "morning after" of the celebration pictured in the Book of Joshua's "night before." Bitter realities begin to set in. The Israelites realize that they are living in a land awash in paganism. They realize that both their military and ideological mastery of the new land is seriously in doubt. Their military dominance of the land is threatened by constant pressures from pagan fiefdoms—from such peoples as the Moabites, the Midianites, the Ammonites and the Canaanites.

What is even more threatening, however, is the subtle "ideological warfare" waged by Baalism against Yahwism. The question of the moment was: Would the Israelite desert religion—the stern faith of the celibate-God Yahweh—survive unaltered in a land dominated by agriculture and the promiscuous gods of fertility?

To begin our discussion of how the Book of Judges answers this question, let us turn to one of the oldest original sources found in the Old Testament, the Song of Deborah and Barak in Jgs 5. This war poem celebrates the victory of a confederacy of several northern Israelite tribes over the Canaanite general Sisera. The poem dates from about 1125 B.C. (The entire period covered by the Book of Judges is approximately 1200-1025 B.C.) The poet, perhaps an eyewitness of the battle, writes:

> "My heart beats fast for Israel's chieftains,
> with those of the people who stood forth boldly,
> For this, bless Yahweh!" (Jgs 5:9)

This poem records for us an early testimony to the Israelites' trust in Yahweh for deliverance from their enemies. The poet's "For this, bless Yahweh!" could well summarize those moments in the early years in Canaan when everything was going right in the Israelites' life—when, as they had been urged repeatedly to do, they put all their trust in Yahweh.

But, sadly, such was not always the case. Instead the Israelites often turned their backs on Yahweh and relied on other gods. What was the result then? As our D editor tells us in Jgs 2:14-15,

> Then Yahweh's anger flamed out against Israel. He handed them over to pillagers who plundered them; he delivered them to the enemies surrounding them, and they were not able to resist them. In every warlike venture, the hand of Yahweh was there to foil them, as Yahweh had warned, as Yahweh had sworn to them. Thus he reduced them to dire distress. (Jgs 2:14-15)

We find in the following verse how Yahweh relieved the people from their periodic distress: "Then Yahweh appointed judges for them, and rescued the men of Israel from the hands of their plunderers" (Jgs 2:16). The Hebrew word used here for "judge" is *shofet*. It has been variously translated by scholars who seek to convey a modern impression of what the word actually means. The translation we will follow in this chapter is *deliverer*. This word suggests what the true role of the "judge" was: not to dispense justice in a legal proceeding as judges do today, but rather to *deliver* the Israelites from a situation of "dire distress."

The judges were ad hoc leaders. That is, they ruled only as long as needed in order to resolve a particular crisis. They were never considered by their followers to be permanent, absolute sovereigns, like the despots and petty kings of the pagans. In fact, the one early Israelite movement toward kingship recorded in the Book of Judges was an abysmal failure. (See the story of Abimelech, Jgs 9.)

Significantly, no judge ever led *all* of the Israelite tribes during his or her (yes, there was a woman among the judges) tenure of leadership. Instead, each judge mentioned was leader in one small area of the land, often at the same time as another judge was leader in a different area. That explains why the sum total of all the ages of the judges listed equals 410 years, while the actual period covered by the book lasted only 175 years.

What is recorded in Judges is a collection of various stories—some from the northern tribes and some from the southern tribes. When the final editor put all of these stories together, the completed version made it appear as if each judge ruled the entire land.

YAHWEH, LEADER OF HIS PEOPLE

It is important to remember that these deliverers were "charismatic" leaders, that is, they were given the *charism* or gift of leadership by Yahweh himself. Yahweh imparted some measure of his own spirit to them in order to empower them for leadership. Thus, it was really Yahweh himself—acting through his handpicked judges—who saved the people from the various crises recorded in Judges.

The true judge was quick to point out that it was *Yahweh* who had brought success. Such was the case with the judge Gideon, for example:

> The men of Israel said to Gideon, "Rule over us, you and your sons and your grandson, because you have rescued us from the power of Midian." But Gideon answered them, "It is not I who shall rule over you, nor my son; Yahweh must be your lord." (Jgs 8:22-23)

In other words, Gideon was saying, "*I* didn't rescue you from the power of the Midianites, *Yahweh* did. Therefore *he* must rule over you."

This notion that it was Yahweh who controlled the appointment of Israel's leaders is extremely important to keep in mind as we proceed through the remainder of the Joshua/Kings saga. Once the people actually *did* accept monarchical rule, the success or failure of a given king was inextricably associated with the man's relationship with

Yahweh (see Chapter Five). If the king had been given Yahweh's spirit, then he and the people prospered. If he had not been given Yahweh's spirit, or if he had originally had this spirit but lost it, he and the people suffered calamity.

This concept of charismatic leadership was based on Israel's belief that Yahweh insisted on relating *directly* with his people and not through intermediaries even when, as we shall see in the next chapter, he allowed them to choose kings as their earthly rulers. Yahweh insisted on *personal* relationship with his people. He had shown this at the Sea of Reeds, repeatedly in the desert, and now in the Promised Land. He was a God who was *in history with* his people. He wanted to be *present* in his people's lives, not distant like the Olympian gods or the nature deities of the Canaanite pagans.

Thus it was that the D editor of Judges constantly asserts the leading role that Yahweh played in the recorded events:

> When Yahweh appointed judges for them, Yahweh was with the judge and rescued them from the hands of their enemies as long as the judge lived, for Yahweh felt pity for them as they groaned under the iron grip of their oppressors. (Jgs 2:18)

Alas, as we read in 2:19, after a particular judge died the people fell quickly back into apostasy.

The core story of Judges is a cycle of infidelity by the people, consequent attack from their enemies, Yahweh's sense of pity, his appointment of a judge and relapse by the people into infidelity after the judge's death. This core story is woven around the life and times of the various judges from Othniel through Samson.

Two editors gave Judges its final form. The final D editor, writing as we have seen in the mid-500's B.C., took the old stories about the various judges and composed Jgs 2—16. Another editor, writing possibly a century *after* D, tacked on the first chapter and Jgs 17—21.

The chapters in this second group aren't really about the judges. They are concerned, rather, with the relationship between the various Israelite tribes at this early stage of their life in the Promised Land. It is anything but a picture of concord and unity. The tribes bicker with each other and even wage a devastating war against one of their number— the tribe of Benjamin (Jgs 19—20).

This accurate portrayal of early Israelite tribal life, based on ancient recollections, illustrates how far the tribes had fallen from the harmonious interrelationship so glowingly depicted in the Book of Joshua. A capsule summary of the sad state of affairs in the Promised Land on the eve of the birth of Samuel is given in three places in

Judges: "In those days there was no king in Israel, and every man did as he pleased" (Jgs 17:6, 19:1, 21:25).

What conclusion shall we draw about the message of the Book of Judges? Is it that kingship was the solution to the discord and disunity which permeated tribal life? As we shall see in 1 Samuel, many people thought that it was. Yet that, as we shall find, was too facile a solution—one fraught with peril.

Were the Israelites so eager to find an easy solution to their problems that, in considering the possibility of kingship, they overlooked the foundation stone of their life as a people? Perhaps they had forgotten who it was who rescued them from Sisera when

"The mountains melted before Yahweh,
before Yahweh, the God of Israel." (Jgs 5:5)

At the conclusion of the era of the judges we find that Israelite life was no different than it had been at the beginning of the period. Enemy armies still attacked on one front and Baalism still threatened on another. No lasting solutions had been found to the problems raised by either peril. Conquest of land by pagan armies and conquest of hearts by pagan gods were both still constant threats.

In the Ephraimite hill country, in the small village of Ramah, a young male baby took his first breath and began to cry. Some who heard the infant's squawking thought perhaps it was a cry of hope for a disunified, discouraged and beleaguered people.

CHAPTER FIVE

'THE LEADER OF MY PEOPLE ISRAEL'

1 and 2 Samuel

I‍t was rare for Yahweh to speak in those days; visions were uncommon. (1 Sm 3:1b)

"Why is God so silent?" we are sometimes tempted to ask. "If only God would do or say something to let me know that he's listening to my prayers, that he cares about my problems!"

Sometimes God seems silent or distant for the same reason that his direct communication with the Israelities was a rare occurrence at the end of the age of the judges. During this period "every man did as he pleased" (Jgs 21:25b) in Israel. There were few who wholeheartedly dedicated themselves to Yahweh, few who surrendered themselves to Yahweh's guidance; thus Yahweh found it impossible to converse with his people directly.

During the last days of the judges, however, Yahweh did raise up for his people someone who was wholeheartedly dedicated to him. And to this person, Yahweh did communicate directly and personally.

In the midst of a period of political and religious crisis, Yahweh heard the prayer of his holy and devout servant Hannah and granted her plea for a son. Hannah called her infant *Samuel* (in Hebrew, "the name of God"). Samuel's purity of devotion to Yahweh provided Yahweh with the opportunity once again to speak directly with his people. It is this man whose name has been given to two Old Testament books: the First Book of Samuel (1 Sm) and the Second Book of Samuel (2 Sm).

Samuel was to serve as a transition figure, bridging the gap between Israel's tribal confederacy and the experiment with monarchy. Likewise, 1 and 2 Samuel serve as a link between Israel's youth and maturity. Before the period of Israelite history recorded in these books, the young nation had struggled to discover its identity among the indigenous peoples in the new homeland. By the conclusion of 2 Samuel, Israel had become a respected kingdom, the dominant power in the land which Yahweh had given.

The young Samuel was dedicated to Yahweh's perpetual service at the temple in Shiloh. He was a man who found favor in Yahweh's eyes and thus was called by Yahweh to reconvert the Israelites to pure Yahweh worship. (See how Yahweh communicated personally with Samuel in 1 Sm 3.)

Samuel began his mission by speaking the word of Yahweh to the priest Eli. Eli's two sons, Phineas and Hophni, had corrupted the Yahweh religion at the Shiloh temple by keeping for themselves the best portions of sacrificial offerings. Since Samuel, in condemning the house of Eli, acted as Yahweh's appointed spokesman, he is thus rightly called a "prophet." Elsewhere in 1 Samuel, he is called a "seer" and a "judge."

Samuel's *principal* role in the drama of 1 and 2 Samuel, however, was to play the part of kingmaker. Samuel anointed Saul as the first king in Israel (c. 1030-1010 B.C.). When Yahweh's spirit departed from Saul, Samuel then anointed as king Saul's successor, David (c. 1010-970 B.C.). But before we consider further the exciting story of Samuel, Saul and David, let us make a brief introductory analysis of the sources and traditions we will be reading in 1 and 2 Samuel.

KINGSHIP AND OTHER LOOSE ENDS IN 1 AND 2 SAMUEL

Even a cursory reading of these books reveals many "loose ends" in the narrative. In fact, we find many statements that are downright contradictory. For example, conflicting answers are given to the question, "Was Yahweh in favor of kingship?" When we read 1 Sm 8; 10:17-27; 12, we find a *negative* treatment of the notion of monarchy. By contrast in 1 Sm 9; 10:1-16; 11, we find kingship presented in a *favorable* light.

Similarly, 1 Sm 9:16 tells us that *Yahweh* himself planted the idea of kingship in Samuel's mind, while an earlier passage (8:7) shows that the idea of kingship originated with the *people* and was characterized by Yahweh as an indication of the people's rejection of him.

A further example of inconsistency is found in 1 Sm 7:13, where we read that in Samuel's early days, "the Philistines were humbled and no longer came into Israelite territory." Why then, a few years later (2 Sm 8), does David have to devote time to driving the Philistines out of the very same Israelite territory? And, "Who killed Saul?" (Contrast 1 Sm 31:4 with 2 Sm 1:10). Finally, to complete our examples, read the highly improbable dual accounts of David's sparing of Saul—one in 1 Sm 24, and the other in 1 Sm 26.

These examples illustrate once again the human dimension of God's revealed Word. If, as some fundamentalists insist, there *is* no human dimension to the Bible—as though God *dictated* Scripture word by word—then we must conclude from our reading of 1 and 2 Samuel that God isn't very smart!

Actually there is an explanation for these discrepancies which threatens neither faith nor reason. It is this: Several writers were at work here. One gives us a tradition which looked upon the monarchy as the best thing that could have ever happened to Israel. Another author, writing at a later date when Israel's experiment with monarchy had proven disastrous, inserted the passages which promoted the anti-monarchy viewpoint.

One of the best examples of this later, anti-monarchy tradition appears in 1 Sm 8:10-22. Here the writer "forewarns" the people of the disadvantages of kingship. It seems obvious, however, that this writer is listing hardships witnessed under an actual king. In fact, the writer describes kingly policies strikingly similar to those of Solomon himself, who reigned nearly three-quarters of a century after the time frame of 1 Sm 8.

The *anti*-monarchist contributor to 1 and 2 Samuel was thus writing from a realistic, pragmatic perspective, putting an *after-the-fact* interpretation of events into the history of the *origins* of kingship. This writer had actually suffered through the bitter realities of Israel's experiment with monarchy. The idealistic *pro*-monarchy contributor, on the other hand, wrote *before the fact*. This optimistic author believed that the selection of a king would be the solution to Israel's problems.

The other discrepancies we looked at above similarly display the work of different hands, writing at different times from different perspectives. Since we could spend an entire book trying to unravel the complex tapestry that is 1 and 2 Samuel, let us simply summarize the generally accepted scholarly viewpoint.

Fragments of several traditions were woven in and through the finished product of 1 and 2 Samuel as we have them today. Some of these were northern-tribe traditions, and some were southern-tribe traditions. (In later chapters we will learn of the north-south split in

Israel which affected so much of the shaping of the Old Testament.) Some were associated with one shrine or holy place, some with another. Each tradition had a different focus on the same core story. Our friend D came along and stitched the various patches of cloth together, sewing in at the same time a healthy piece of Deuteronomic theology (for example, 1 Sm 2:27-36 and 2 Sm 7).

One bit of writing which D handed down to us virtually unaltered is 2 Sm 9—20, often called the "Court History of David." In that segment we have a true historical record, probably written by an eyewitness possessed of keen powers of observation and remarkably astute psychological insight. Since this writer preceded by some five centuries the famous Greek historian Herodotus—who is usually called "Father of History"—we might consider the writer of 2 Sm 9—20 to be the *true* father of history. The identity of this writer is shrouded in anonymity, but we owe him a tremendous debt of gratitude for leaving behind the remarkable story of the great king David, the man who was the apple of Yahweh's eye and the foundation stone of the later Jewish hope for a Messiah.

But that gets a little ahead of our story. Before we can consider the saga of one of history's greatest political and religious geniuses, the great son of Jesse from Bethlehem, we must return to the more mundane and tragic story of his predecessor, the wretched and pitiable Saul.

SAUL: ISRAEL'S FIRST KING

Saul didn't ask to be king. By one account (1 Sm 9) he was out looking for his father's lost asses when suddenly this rather impetuous character (Samuel) ran up and anointed him king over the chosen people of the God who rules the entire universe. How would *we* have handled such an awesome responsibility? Probably not any better than Saul did. Let's look at one of Saul's blunders.

Saul had waged "holy war" against the Amalekites. He had been told by Yahweh's mouthpiece, Samuel, to "put under the ban" all that the Amalekites possessed—that is, to destroy the people and everything they owned *completely*.

What would *we* have done? Perhaps we would have protested, "Look, Lord, we've beaten the Amalekites. Isn't that enough? Do we *really* have to slaughter every man, woman, child, ox and sheep, camel and donkey?" (See 1 Sm 15:3.)

That was a question that may have passed through Saul's mind. At any rate, he decided to keep aside the *best* of the animals and to offer them in sacrifice to Yahweh. This brought about Saul's downfall. Samuel found out what Saul had done and became furious. Through Samuel, Yahweh himself spoke these words of condemnation:

> "Is the pleasure of Yahweh in holocausts and sacrifices
> or in *obedience* to the voice of Yahweh?" (1 Sm 15:22)

As we would say in today's jargon, Saul "blew it." He substituted his own judgment, his own thoughts, for those of Yahweh. That finished him as king. Yahweh had to have as king someone who would be steadfastly—even *minutely*—loyal to his will. Why? *Yahweh* was leader of these people, not the king. That was the point they could never get straight.

Yahweh *loved* his people. He wanted to be their God. He wanted to go before them in battle, win their wars for them and deliver their enemies into their hands. He wanted to be *Yahweh Sabaoth* ("Lord God of Hosts"), the protector and defender of his people. How could he be this if an upstart like Saul kept getting in the way, trying to run the show *for* Yahweh? After the sad experience with Saul, Yahweh asked, "Whom will I choose to be the leader of my people Israel?"

DAVID: THE APPLE OF GOD'S EYE

We all know the answer to the above question. Yahweh found a young shepherd, "a boy of fresh complexion, with fine eyes and pleasant bearing" (1 Sm 16:22) named David. (Since the name means *commander*, it is possible that David's boyhood name may have been something else. Possibly his early name simply merged with the title at a later date.)

As we read the story of David in 1 and 2 Samuel we should keep in mind the familiar dictum that "history is written from the point of view of the winners." This more than anything else accounts for David's "good press" and Saul's "bad press." Saul has come down to us as a tragic, even detestable figure, while David is everyone's favorite biblical hero. Saul erred in judgment and Yahweh deposed him. David sinned grievously and managed to return to God's favor. Wherein lies the difference? More than likely only in the simple human prejudice which glorifies the memory of those who are successful and vilifies those who can't get things done. In biblical literature as in art, the portrait of David has come down to us with the positive features exaggerated and the negative features hidden or ignored.

For example, it is difficult to dismiss from one's mind the heroic image of the young David given to us by the great Michelangelo. Yet in reality David was probably a rather ordinary-looking country lad, not a classical Greek athlete. Remember, Samuel himself had to be told by Yahweh to overlook one of Jesse's more appealing sons: "Take no notice of his appearance or his height for I have rejected him," Yahweh said of David's brother Eliab. "God does not see as man sees; man looks at appearances but Yahweh looks at the heart" (1 Sm 16:7).

It was David's heart which attracted Yahweh to the young shepherd, and it was David's heart which Yahweh was to hold up to his people in future years as the model of devotion, loyalty and service. Nowhere in the Old Testament do we find a heart more steadfast in its love of Yahweh than the heart of David. This steadfastness, this purity of love, this single-hearted affection for Yahweh best symbolized the relationship Yahweh wanted to have with *all* of his people. For this reason David and his age came to be regarded by most successive Old Testament writers as the model of virtue and religion.

David's greatness of soul shone through even in his moment of great sin. His adultery with Bathsheba and his conspiracy to murder her husband Uriah (2 Sm 11) were followed by a heart-wrenching act of pure and sincere repentance. David's swift remorse (12:13-17) was not contrived. He had shown himself on several occasions to be keenly aware of the presence of Yahweh in his life, whether in spontaneous dance before the Ark of the Covenant as it was carried into Jerusalem (2 Sm 6) or, as here, in immediate response to Nathan's brutal chastisement. David's trust in Yahweh's love was not destroyed by his sin, and in that we see, perhaps, his greatest characteristic.

David knew at once what he had to do. He humbled himself before Yahweh and reestablished the relationship which he had broken. The verses of Psalm 51 reflect the inner workings of David's spirit, showing a man who understood fully both the destructive power of sin and the certainty of Yahweh's forgiveness. David was confident that Yahweh would not scorn his crushed and broken heart.

David's path to the throne had not been an easy one. In the chapters of 1 Samuel following David's anointing by Samuel, we find that—to vary a remark by Thomas Edison—David earned the kingship with "98 percent perspiration and 2 percent inspiration." This may seem surprising since we are told that "the spirit of Yahweh seized on David and...left Saul" (1 Sm 16:13, 14). Yet we discover that David still had to struggle hard actually to assume his kingly office. Again, several traditions were at work in 1 and 2 Samuel. Even though David had been anointed by Samuel, as one tradition tells us, his actual accession to the throne, another tradition points out, still depended on the resolution of several thorny problems.

Of these problems the two greatest were (1) Saul's insane jealousy and attempt to eradicate his young rival and (2) the threat from the Philistines. Until these two problems were resolved, neither David nor the tribes he hoped to lead would have a moment's peace. The story of Saul's intrigues and his eventual undoing are skillfully and movingly narrated in 1 Sm 18—2 Sm 1:16. The purpose of these passages is to illustrate both how clever David was in eluding Saul's grasp and how intent Yahweh was on bringing David to victory and to power.

The Philistine threat posed perhaps an even greater challenge to David than Saul's murderous scheming. The Philistines represented the greatest military threat the Israelites had yet faced. These "sea people" had settled in the Mediterranean coastal area of Palestine at about the same time as Joshua and his followers crossed the Jordan. The Israelite thrust westward and the Philistine expansion eastward soon exploded into a conflict that threatened Israel's very existence.

The Philistines formed a five-city coalition (Gaza, Ashkelon, Ashdod, Gath and Ekron), similar in nature to the Israelite tribal confederacy. The Philistines were master ironworkers, whereas the Israelites were by and large unskilled at this craft. As a result the Philistine army, with its sophisticated chariots, spears and javelins, won victory after victory.

It was largely because of the Philistine threat that Israel opted for kingship in the first place. The tribal elders realized that their loose confederacy and their previous reliance on ad hoc judges to lead them into battle would have to be replaced with a more effective form of government. What was needed in this life-and-death struggle with the Philistines was *lasting unity*. Perhaps it was the Philistine threat which also contributed to David's rise and Saul's decline. As the women of Israel sang,

> "Saul has killed his thousands,
> and David his tens of thousands." (1 Sm 18:7)

The tribal chieftains likewise realized that it was David who was the better general. David's military acumen and his skill at political organizing saved the day.

Although we don't know the entire story, somehow David introduced the Israelite forces to chariot fighting and other "modern" inventions of warfare. By the time of David's son Solomon, the Israelite army was well-accustomed to chariot warfare (see 1 Kgs 10:26-29).

Perhaps because of the gravity of the Philistine threat and the terror which this threat had impressed upon Israelite memories, we are given only a one-sentence description of David's eventual subjugation of the Philistines: "After this, David defeated the Philistines and subdued them" (2 Sm 8:1).

David's acceptance as king by the tribes had occurred in two stages: The first stage was his acceptance by the southern tribes (2 Sm 2:1-4) and the second his acceptance by the northern tribes (2 Sm 5:1-5). David's reign was thus the first period of government to unify all the tribes of Israel. David—the southerner from Judah—reigned as king over the unified northern and southern tribes for 33 years.

Since the "Court History of David" is so eloquently and accurately set forth for us in 2 Sm 9—20, we need dwell no further on it here, except to look at one last concept: the covenant Yahweh made with David—presented in 2 Sm 7, one of the key passages in all the Old Testament. Turn to that passage now and read it in its entirety.

THE DAVIDIC COVENANT

As we have seen, one of the central teachings of 1 and 2 Samuel is that Yahweh desired to relate to his people personally and directly. Yahweh made it clear from the start of his relationship with the Israelites that he would not be a distant god. Rather, as Yahweh was eager to demonstrate, he would intervene in history on the side of his people as no pagan god had ever done or was capable of doing. Yahweh himself would take the initiative to live among his people. This predisposition on the part of Yahweh to remain near to them is what underlies Yahweh's refusal, as described in 2 Sm 7, to allow David to build a temple.

A temple, Yahweh seems to say, would be a possible first step by which the Israelites would distance themselves from Yahweh, and by which they would formalize and ritualize an otherwise intimate and personal relationship. Yahweh wanted no institution or structure to come between him and his people. Thus in 7:6-11, David is reminded by Yahweh how, throughout Israel's history, he has intervened directly and personally on their behalf. He stresses that the only thing David needs to be successful is reliance on Yahweh's personal guidance and protection.

As final assurance of Yahweh's personal direction of his people, Yahweh instructs David that the only "house" Yahweh wants to live in is the "house" (dynasty) of David's own family—and not in a temple.

"Your House and your sovereignty will always stand secure before me and your throne be established forever," Yahweh tells David through Nathan (2 Sm 7:16).

Yahweh's promise to keep David's throne secure forever became the basis for the later Jewish hope for and belief in a messiah. Notice that the promise we encounter in this passage is an unconditional one—Yahweh places no obligations on David for the fulfillment of this promise. Yahweh freely and unconditionally binds himself to preserve the house of David forever and to raise up a descendant of David whose rule will be perpetual. It is important to keep in mind the unconditional nature of this covenant with the house of David as we move into 1 and 2 Kings.

This Davidic Covenant would become more and more important as Israel watched the disintegration of the unified kingdom which Solomon inherited from his father, David. In fact, this covenant would at one point become the last slender reed of hope for the Israelites to grasp as they struggled to stay afloat in the whirlpool of chaos and catastrophe which characterized the latter days of their kingdom. But before we reach that sad moment, we must first consider the moment of greatness when Israel seemed most blessed among all the peoples on earth: the story of Solomon in all his glory.

CHAPTER SIX

'SOLOMON IN ALL HIS GLORY'

1 and 2 Kings, Genesis

Judah and Israel were like sand by the sea for number; they ate and drank and lived happily. (1 Kgs 4:20)

Have you ever heard people talk about the "good old days"? Perhaps you yourself have a pleasant memory of some former period of your life which suggests a time of comfort and peace lived in the pleasant company of supportive friends. In your imagination you remember it as a time free of anxieties, tensions and worries.

We all know that there really aren't any "good old days." We know those days had some "bad" mixed in as well. Yet, there do appear to be times—in our personal history as well as in the history of an entire people—which stand out as truly fortunate and blessed. In the memory of the ancient Israelites, the period which best represents the "good old days" was the half-century that spanned the last years of King David's reign through the end of the reign of King Solomon—approximately 980-930 B.C.

During this era, Israel enjoyed a respite from foreign attack. Her enemies were preoccupied with civil wars, rebellions and other domestic problems. On the home front King David and then King Solomon eliminated all rivals to their respective thrones. They were thus able to terminate the bloody factionalism and strife which had so often characterized Israelite tribal life. For once, if only briefly, the tribes stood united—first under David and then under Solomon—in a common purpose.

We gain an understanding of this common purpose by reading the passages in 1 Kings which are devoted to the reign of King Solomon. As we read these passages (1 Kgs 3—11), let us keep in mind the ancient Israelite theory of kingship: The king was thought to "stand for" the people before Yahweh. The king expressed in his person the entire body of the Israelites.

Thus, in telling the story of Solomon and of his successors in 1 and 2 Kings, our Deuteronomic historian is telling us at the same time the personal stories of *all* the Israelites. If a king was righteous and faithful to Yahweh—like David—then *all* the people were considered faithful, and all were blessed. Similarly, if a given king was unfaithful he and the people as well suffered Yahweh's punishment. This ancient way of thinking, no matter how foreign to our contemporary view, is necessary to understand the biblical presentation of Israel's history.

RELIGION—ISRAEL'S BUSINESS

The very essence of the Israelite kingdom was its *theocratic* nature. A theocracy is a form of government in which there is no separation between politics and religion because the head of state is presumed to be ruling at God's direct command. The concept of theocracy perfectly summarizes the Israelite national purpose during those good old days of David and Solomon.

If, as Calvin Coolidge once said, "the business of America is business," then the "business" of ancient Israel was religion. More specifically, the national purpose of Israel was to attend to the relationship with Yahweh—which, as we have seen, had been forged in the desert and solemnized by the covenant at Mt. Sinai. In this relationship Yahweh was the true leader of his people; the king was simply his earthly representative who, it was hoped, would serve Yahweh's interests and safeguard his covenant. If the king wavered in his responsibility, the people and the nation were put in peril.

As we read the Deuteronomic history of Solomon's reign, we find our D editor teaching us that *true* theocratic rule brought great prosperity to the nation. Our D historian thus paints a lavish picture in 1 Kgs 3—11 of the blessings which Yahweh would give his people when their king remained faithful and submitted his life to Yahweh's control. Solomon (and thus the nation) was blessed with great wisdom and wealth because of his fidelity to Yahweh. His kingdom expanded; the former desert nomads even developed a navy! Riches, fame, prestige and honor all flowed into Jerusalem.

All of this wisdom and wealth was secondary to the primary blessing—and event—of Solomon's reign: the building and consecration of the temple at Jerusalem. Our D historian assures us that *because* of Yahweh's permanent presence among his people in the temple and *because* of Solomon's fidelity to Yahweh, Israel received all the material blessings recounted in 1 Kgs 3—11.

Since the Jerusalem temple was such an important aspect both of D's theology and of later *Jewish* theology, it would be wise to stop for a moment and read 1 Kgs 8, which describes the transportation of the Ark of the Covenant to the new temple and Solomon's dedication ceremony. The purpose of 1 Kgs 8:1-13 is to describe two important ways in which Yahweh manifested his presence among his people.

The first of these was the Ark of the Covenant. The Ark was a tangible, material focal point for the presence of God. It was a box made of acacia wood, four feet long, four feet deep, and two and a half feet wide. In it were kept the tablets on which the Ten Commandments were written. A plate of gold on top was said to be the seat from which Yahweh dispensed his mercy.

The second way Yahweh showed his presence was the dark cloud which, in contrast to the Ark, was intangible and nonmaterial. As a symbol, the cloud thus emphasized the transcendent, limitless nature of Yahweh. Whereas one could capture the essence of the pagan gods by reducing them to forms of stone, wood or other natural elements, Yahweh could not be so described or defined.

Previously, the Ark had been carried about from place to place at the whim of circumstance. Now it would be assured of stability. Yahweh could at last rest securely among his people. In effect, the ceremony of 1 Kgs 8 amounted to a final verification by Yahweh of the Israelites as his chosen people and of Jerusalem as his dwelling place. The long years of transience were over. The two ancient expressions of Yahweh's holy presence are finally manifested together in a permanent physical dwelling. In 8:12 Solomon marvels at the mysterious transcendence of Yahweh and, in 8:13, at the fact that Yahweh has allowed Solomon to be the instrument for providing the temple as Yahweh's permanent dwelling.

In the remaining verses of 1 Kgs 8 our D editor, writing in the mid-500's B.C., develops for us his standard theological teaching: that fidelity to Yahweh's covenant brings blessing while infidelity brings disaster. This insistence on the conditionality of the Sinai Covenant is as aspect of D's theology which is now familiar to us. Notice, however, that in 1 Kgs 8 two new wrinkles are added.

The first appears in 8:25, where Solomon gives his own

rendition of the promise Yahweh made to David in 2 Sm 7. As Solomon remembers it, Yahweh promised David:

> "You shall never lack for a man to sit before me on the throne of Israel, if only your sons are careful how they behave, walking before me as you yourself have done." (1 Kgs 8:25)

What D is doing here is taking the unconditional Davidic Covenant of 2 Sm 7 and appropriating it into his own theology.

Although D is not downplaying the *certainty of fulfillment* of this covenant, he *is* nonetheless inserting a subtle deviation into Yahweh's promise to David. That deviation contains a noticeable element of "iffiness": *If* the kings who follow David don't emulate David's fidelity to Yahweh, they are in big trouble.

This, of course, is in keeping with one of D's main purposes in writing the entire Joshua/Kings unit. He wanted to show *why* the nation eventually fell. The answer is planted in seed form in 1 Kgs 8: If the kings (people) are faithful (like David), they will prosper; if they are not, they are doomed. That is why throughout 1 and 2 Kings, D measures the careers of all Judahite kings who come after David by David's *model* conduct.

The second "new wrinkle" to D's theology is evident in Solomon's dedication prayer:

> "Day and night let your eyes watch over this house, over this *place* of which you have said, 'My name shall be there.' "
> (1 Kgs 8:29, emphasis added)

In this verse we see D's concern to emphasize the Jerusalem temple as the locus, the *center* of the Israelite religion. In 1 Kgs 11:13, D goes so far as to elevate Jerusalem to the same level of importance as David himself when it comes to stating the reason for Yahweh's mercy in preserving the dynasty of Solomon:

> "For the sake of my servant David, and for the sake of *Jerusalem which I have chosen,*" Yahweh says, "I will leave your son one tribe."
> (1 Kgs 11:13, emphasis added)

This emphasis on Jerusalem as the center of worship becomes a major thrust of D's theology in 1 and 2 Kings. We see the reason for this as the story of the various kings develops. Time after time the kings fall into apostasy, tolerating and even encouraging worship of the pagan gods on the "high places." These high places were outlying shrines where the people—including some Israelite priests—found it all too easy to mix elements of the Yahweh faith with elements of Baalism or other pagan cults.

As a result, D—who believed generally in *extreme* corrective measures—called for the eradication of *all* non-Jerusalem worship. By doing this, he thought, the Judahite kings and the Jerusalem clergy could keep a close watch over the official state religion, making sure pagan practices did not creep into the Yahweh faith. D's insistence on Jerusalem as *the* site of Yahweh worship took on even more significance after the political and religious schism which followed Solomon's death.

Before taking up that story, however, we must look at one more important feature of the "glory days" of Israel: a piece of biblical literature which has survived while the trappings and splendor of the monarchy have long faded. This literary achievement is the epic of the Yahwist, the source to whom we have assigned the initial J in previous chapters.

THE YAHWIST AND HIS EPIC

The existence of J's work is in itself something of an exception. For, aside from another work of literature—the secular history known as the Court History of David—ancient Israel left us little in the way of cultural achievements. This is because ancient Israel, as we have seen, was a theocracy.

Since the nation was focused so singularly on religion, it had no time for many aspects of culture which were so important to other ancient peoples. We find no remains of an indigenous Israelite art or architecture, no works of sculpture and no music or literature that were purely secular—that is, unrelated to the Israelite worship of Yahweh. This was partially due to the proscription against "graven images" and idols found in the Law. It is further due to the tendency in theocracies to devote a good deal of intellectual energy to religion and very little to secular pursuits.

The identity of the Yahwist (in English, called "J," after the German spelling of Yahweh—*Jahweh*) is unknown to us. All we know is that he probably wrote his great epic toward the end of Solomon's reign. As we have seen, this period in Israel's history was characterized by marvelous events—the unification of the tribes, the Davidic Covenant and the spread of Israelite fame and prestige to the far corners of the ancient world. In a period such as this when Israel enjoyed peace on every side, a great writer could find both time and inspiration to compose great literature. The Yahwist took advantage of the situation in Israel to do just that.

His *motive* in writing was to explain why and how Israel had risen to greatness, so that future generations would know the story of Israel's past. His *purpose* was to demonstrate how Yahweh had been at work from the first day of creation through the time of Moses, forming the Israelites into a special people, into Yahweh's holy people. The Yahwist's *method* was to illustrate how Yahweh's plan to raise his people to greatness unfolded through the various events of history, beginning with Adam and Eve and extending to the final days of the Israelite desert community.

Where did the Yahwist get his ideas? Like any great writer, the Yahwist was a keen observer of the society in which he lived. He knew the great oral tales of Israel's past which had circulated among his people for generations. Further, he recognized the aspects of his own culture which posed threats to the Israelite religious tradition. The Yahwist feared that his contemporaries would forget who had been responsible for their present greatness. He wanted to make sure that his readers never lost sight of the dominant role that Yahweh played both in forming the people and in bringing them to the pinnacle of success in Solomon's time.

Therefore, J took the great tales of Israel's past and organized them in such a way as to highlight or emphasize Yahweh's great deeds on behalf of his people. J also wanted to show that Yahweh intended his people to play a leading role in the *salvation*—there's no better word for it—of *other* peoples. Thus he begins his account of Yahweh's action in history not with the Israelites, but with Adam—the progenitor of the human race. Yahweh was the *universal* God who picked the Israelites as his special people so they, in turn, could bring blessings to *all* the people on earth.

It is beyond the scope of this book to present a detailed analysis of which passages in the Pentateuch (the first five books of the Bible) were written by J, as opposed to other sources. I have given an example in Chapter One of how these sources were woven together in a certain passage in Exodus. Scholars have made the same type of analysis of the remainder of Exodus, as well as of the other books of the Pentateuch. Their findings appear in various commentaries on the Bible, as well as in certain annotated versions of the Bible. Therefore if you would like to read all of J's verses straight through in Genesis without stopping to read the P or E verses, I refer you to a good commentary or annotated Bible (such as the *Jerusalem Bible* or the annotated *Revised Standard Version*) which will separate the various traditions for you. For *our* purposes, it will be sufficient to describe the *general* features of J's epic without listing all the chapters or verses which are J's.

Since we have seen that J started with Adam, obviously the place to begin our discussion of J's epic is in the Book of Genesis (Gn). J's account in Genesis begins in Gn 2:4b ("b" means the second half of 2:4): "At the time when Yahweh God made earth and heaven...." The J account continues through Gn 11. (Gn 1:1—2:4a, "In the beginning...," was P's contribution, as we shall discuss in a later chapter.)

In these 10 chapters of Genesis J develops his principal theological theme: Humanity obedient and submissive to Yahweh lives in peace and happiness; humanity trusting in its own devices brings disaster down upon its head. This theme is woven in and through the stories of Adam and Eve, Cain and Abel, Noah and his descendants. At every step in this early journey of humankind, Yahweh intervenes to punish disobedience and to call sinful humanity back to him.

The conflict between wholehearted fidelity to Yahweh and religious syncretism was present in the human soul right from the start, J tells his contemporary readers. Adam's banishment from Eden, Cain's exile, the destruction of the world by flood in Noah's time were all means Yahweh used to punish the first prototypes of infidelity. In the same way Yahweh used the chastising sword of the Philistines and other foreign aggressors during the time in which J lived and wrote to punish contemporary infidelity.

That was the bad news. The good news was that Yahweh contrived from the start to deliver the human family from the desperate straits into which it had fallen through its disobedience. In other words, Yahweh had planned an "out," a way to escape from the disastrous effects of sin. To do this, Yahweh chose a man named Abram and said to him:

> "All the tribes of the earth
> shall bless themselves by you." (Gn 12:3b)

J thus prepared his readers for the *universal mission* which the Israelites were to undertake to bring salvation to *all* of fallen humanity—a mission which would come into clearer focus some 400 years after J's time in the writings of the mysterious "Second-Isaiah" (see Chapter Eight).

J next presents the account of Yahweh's *special covenant* with Abram, later renamed Abraham:

> "To your descendants I give this land from the wadi of Egypt to the Great River." (Gn 15:18)

61

Those descendants, Yahweh said, would be as numerous as the stars in heaven. By this J is reminding his audience that it was Yahweh who planned, centuries ago in Abraham's time, to bring his people into possession of the Promised Land. And the Davidic Covenant, so prominent in Israelite consciousness in J's time, was a means of fulfilling the Abrahamic Covenant of long ago. The implication for J's audience was clear: All along the way, from Abraham to David, Yahweh had led, guided, planned, promised and fulfilled his promises.

Even when hope seemed lost, Yahweh intervened to carry out his plan of salvation. Sarah's and Rebekah's sterility were no obstacle to Yahweh (Gn 18 and 25). The promise to Abraham had to be kept, and thus Yahweh gave children to barren women. Yahweh even used the jealousy and deceit of Jacob's sons to effect his plan (Gn 37—50). Joseph, sold into slavery by his brothers, is raised by Yahweh to the position of prime minister of Egypt. Yahweh thus turns the tables on Joseph's betrayers, who must rely on Joseph for rescue from famine.

All of this is done to work out Yahweh's plan. What *looks like* a desperate situation for the tribe of Jacob is turned by Yahweh into triumph, all for the purpose of forming his people and bringing them to the land he had promised Abraham.

J continues his epic in Exodus and Numbers with the same purpose and method. Yahweh continues to guide, lead, correct infidelity and offer his recalcitrant people chance after chance for reconciliation. Yahweh's purpose throughout is to bring his people to the Promised Land, so that they can begin to assert themselves as the people by whom "all tribes of the earth" shall become blessed.

Quite a story, and quite a cultural achievement! J's epic must have made a tremendous impression on his first readers, those Israelites in Solomon's time who justly took pride in their newly won fame and fortune. Yet at the same time, J's epic must have had a humbling effect on his audience. No devout Israelite could have read it without realizing the insignificance of human achievement and the predominance of Yahweh's role in bringing the nation to its present position of greatness.

CHAPTER SEVEN

'WHAT SHARE HAVE WE IN DAVID?'

1 and 2 Kings, Genesis

The history of the 400-year period covered in 1 and 2 Kings (Kgs) is varied and complex. Our D historian didn't even try to present every event and happening. His concern was primarily to present the *theological significance* of this four-century history. D refers readers interested in an in-depth treatment of the history of the period to "The Book of the Annals of the Kings of Israel" (1 Kgs 14:19), "The Book of the Annals of the Kings of Judah" (1 Kgs 15:7), and "The Book of the Acts of Solomon" (1 Kgs 11:41). These three sources are lost to us, but it is obvious that D made great use of them and of other preexisting sources in putting together his final edition of 1 and 2 Kings, sometime in the mid-500's B.C.

Since we, like D, are more concerned with the theological significance of the events which occurred during that four-century span of time, we likewise will not dwell too heavily on historical details. The approach we will use will be first to look at the *broad outline* of *what* happened, and then to consider D's judgment as to *why* it happened. We will do this in two chapters: This chapter covers the period from the death of Solomon (c. 931 B.C.) to the fall of Samaria (721 B.C.). Chapter Eight will cover the history of Judah from the reign of King Hezekiah (716-687 B.C.) to the fall of Jerusalem in 587 B.C.

You may have noticed in the previous paragraphs some new terminology, such as *Israel, Judah* and *Samaria*. The reason is that we will now be dealing with two new and distinct political entities—the northern kingdom of *Israel* and the southern kingdom of *Judah*.

Before we proceed we need to define our new terms. The first new definition will be the meaning of the word *Israel*. Heretofore, it referred to *all* the Israelite tribes living in Palestine. That usage will now change. In this chapter and the next two chapters, *Israel* will refer only to the 10 northern tribes who separated from the House of David in the year 931 B.C. (*Samaria* was the name given to the capital of this northern kingdom.) The remaining southern tribes, whose capital was Jerusalem, will now be referred to as *Judah*.

THE DESTRUCTION OF DAVIDIC UNITY

The account of this split between north and south is presented in 1 Kgs 12. The reason for the split—according to D—was that Solomon in his later years departed from strict fidelity to Yahweh. In 1 Kgs 11, we see what precipitated Solomon's eventual demise: his inordinate number of wives, most of whom were foreigners—two violations of the Deuteronomic moral code (Dt 17:17; 7:3-4).

While this situation probably existed from the start of Solomon's reign, D apparently did not feel that it threatened Solomon's single-hearted devotion to Yahweh until old age, when Solomon was convinced by his wives to turn to other gods (1 Kgs 11:4). This probably meant only that he tolerated his wives' imported pagan rites and allowed foreign traders to practice their pagan religion while in Israel on business. There is no evidence that Solomon himself became a devotee of pagan gods, or that he actively weakened pure devotion to Yahweh at the temple in Jerusalem.

Nevertheless, Solomon's tolerant attitude fell short of strict compliance with the model conduct established by David. Thus, according to D, God wrenched the kingdom away from Solomon. Notice that Solomon's failure to maintain the high standards set by David is mentioned twice (11:4, 6), and that the only reason God did not completely dispossess Solomon and his son was because of David's loyalty (11:12—13). God's fidelity to the promise he made to David (2 Sm 7:16) was the unfailing banner of faith which D held up before his readers.

Solomon's son, Rehoboam, arrogantly and quickly blundered into political schism (1 Kgs 12:1-16). The northern tribes, who perhaps were looking for any excuse to rid themselves of harsh policies instituted by Solomon, replied to Rehoboam's arrogance by saying,

"What share have we in David?
We have no inheritance in the son of Jesse.

64

To your tents, Israel!
Henceforth look after your own house, David!" (1 Kgs 12:16)

In other words, "You southerners mind your own business and leave us northerners alone!" These northern tribes thus rejected Solomon's successor and chose their own king, Jeroboam. From this point on, *Israel* refers to this new political entity.

Our D historian saw King Jeroboam of Israel as the apotheosis of wickedness. As a result, D will constantly refer to Jeroboam as the model of infidelity and evil in the same way that he will constantly refer to David as the model of fidelity and virtue. All future kings of Judah will be judged by the standard of David and all future kings of Israel will be judged by the standard of Jeroboam.

As you might expect in such a methodology, all the Israelite kings are soundly condemned by D; only Judahite kings are praised. D is thus definitely pro-Judah and anti-Israel in his writing.

The reason is clear. Yahweh's promise in 2 Sm 7 was made to David and his descendants. Thus only those descendants could advance Yahweh's plan to keep the Davidic throne secure forever. D saw the northern kings, who were outside of David's line, as illegitimate usurpers. D thus spared no abuse and invective in condemning them because they stood in the way of Yahweh's plan.

Since D regarded the dastardly Jeroboam as the model of Israelite wickedness, let us consider for a moment how it was that Jeroboam sinned.

In 1 Kgs 12:26-33 we find that, once chosen king, Jeroboam quickly moved to provide the 10 northern tribes with religious centers of their own. This was wise *political* strategy. Religious pilgrims regularly going from Israel to Judah could not be expected to distinguish for long between Jerusalem (the site of the temple) as religious center and Jerusalem as national capital.

Jeroboam undoubtedly did not intend to start a new religion by setting up shrines in Bethel and Dan. Nor were the golden calves (12:28) intended to be new gods. They were probably intended only to represent Yahweh's throne, somewhat similar to the function of the golden covering on the Ark or the cherubim above it.

The symbol of the two calves was too confusing, however, and many people undoubtedly mistook Jeroboam's actions to mean that he regarded Yahweh on a par with Baal, whose physical image was a bull. In fact, after a period of time, many people made no distinction at all between Yahweh and Baal. Thus, whatever Jeroboam's motives and intentions may have been, D placed the responsibility for Israel's subsequent apostasy squarely on Jeroboam's shoulders.

Beginning with the reign of Jeroboam in Israel (931-910) and of Rehoboam in Judah (931-913) the tragic effects of political and religious schism gradually manifested themselves. Israel fell deeper and deeper into apostasy.

The House of Jeroboam in Israel was succeeded by the House of Omri. King Omri (885-874) bought certain property in Israel on which to build his new capital city, Samaria (1 Kgs 16:24). Omri's son Ahab (874-853), like his predecessors in office, tolerated the practice of Baalism in Israel.

ELIJAH: SHOWDOWN WITH BAALISM

Ahab's reign is noteworthy less because of what *he* did than because of his *relationship* with two stronger characters who overshadow him in our drama: Ahab's wife Jezebel and the fiery prophet of Yahweh whose very name—*Eli-jah*—means "Yahweh is my God."

The story of the prophet Elijah was drawn by D from an independent source called the "Elijah Cycle." This Cycle is found in 1 Kgs 17—19, 21, and 2 Kgs 1:1-18. Since the Elijah Cycle provides excellent theological commentary on the history of the times, and since it forms a necessary prelude to our discussion of the "classical prophets" in Chapter Nine, let us consider it in closer detail.

The historical setting of the Elijah Cycle is the reign of King Ahab. Ahab's father, King Omri, had arranged for young Ahab to marry the Phoenician princess Jezebel, daughter of Ethbaal, King of Tyre. When Ahab assumed the throne, Jezebel immediately embarked on an ambitious program to convert the Israelites to the worship of the patron god of Tyre, Baal-Melkart.

Ahab meekly supported his foreign wife. He built a temple to Baal and permitted cultic sacrifices to be performed on Baal's altar. Ahab himself was not rejecting Yahweh. He was merely trying, for reasons of politics and economics, to keep Jezebel and her Phoenician entourage satisfied. Yahweh, however, moved quickly to prevent this movement toward religious syncretism. He commissioned Elijah to call Ahab and the people back to single-hearted devotion.

The stage for the conflict with Baal is set in 1 Kgs 17:1. Elijah challenged Baal in Baal's very stronghold—the sphere of fertility—by calling forth a drought in the land. With the challenged issued, Elijah retired to the desert (17:2-6), relying solely on Yahweh to strengthen him for his upcoming confrontation with the prophets of Baal. In the meantime the drought slowly began to ravage the land—the land over which Baal was supposedly almighty lord and which he alone, supposedly, could keep rich and fertile.

After some time, during which the drought had taken a severe toll, Yahweh told Elijah that it was time to call the people to return to him with single-hearted devotion. Elijah's confrontation with Baal and his prophets was to be carried out in successive stages, culminating in Elijah's triumph on Mt. Carmel.

Yahweh Gives Food in the Midst of Drought

The first stage in this confrontation occurred in Zarephath in Phoenicia—Baal's own province, where he was wholeheartedly worshiped. In 17:7-16, Elijah used a widow's extreme poverty as a means of confronting Baal. If Baal could not provide enough wheat and oil to one of his own followers, his supposed power would have in reality been no power at all. Yahweh promises that the widow's meager supply of grain and oil will last through the drought—and it does! The point of the miracle is that Yahweh is Lord over all nature. Yahweh's power was effective even in the very stronghold of Baal. The latter was powerless to provide food to his own followers, while Yahweh mercifully fed even those who worshiped Baal.

Yahweh Defeats the Prophets of Baal

Having successfully demonstrated to one of Baal's devotees that it is Yahweh who controls life and death, Elijah next directly challenged the prophets of Baal on Mt. Carmel. Elijah's rebuke of the people (18:20) suggests the ambivalence which the simultaneous worship of Yahweh and Baal had produced in the religious life of the time. The people, like a bird hopping on one foot and then another, tried to straddle separate branches. Elijah wanted to make it clear that worship of Yahweh and worship of Baal were mutually exclusive. Jezebel's program of establishing the Baal cult had evidently met with great success, for Elijah emphasized that a decision for Yahweh had to be made *now*, before the people became thoroughly converted to Baalism.

The contest was really between monotheism, as represented by Elijah and the Yahweh cult, and the polytheistic Baalism prevalent throughout Palestine. Elijah's quiet confidence in Yahweh, underscored by his mocking of Baal (18:27), is juxtaposed against the frenetic anxiety of the Baal prophets, who resorted to gashing themselves in order to stir their deity to action (18:28).

Elijah calmly rebuilt the altar of Yahweh, probably destroyed by

Jezebel, and, by thoroughly soaking the altar with water, set up a situation in which Yahweh's intervention would be made unmistakably clear to all. The people's response to this display of power (18:39) shows that Elijah had scored a victory for monotheism. Yahweh is not simply *stronger* than the god Baal. Rather, "Yahweh is God," purely and simply.

Yahweh Ends the Great Drought

The climax of the story of Elijah's challenge to Baalism occurred as Yahweh ended the great drought, thereby demonstrating conclusively that it is he who controls rain, fertility and the powers of nature.

Elijah's last act in the drama was to beseech Yahweh for rain. Assuming a posture of submission to Yahweh (18:42), Elijah directed his servant to look for a sign of Yahweh's termination of the drought (18:43). Eventually a small storm cloud formed on the horizon (18:44). Elijah ended his prayer, and the rain began to fall in torrents.

The message of the entire episode of the drought is that Yahweh is a jealous God who will not permit his people to worship the gods of the nations. Further, he will intervene directly to call his people back to single-hearted devotion whenever they waver. While he used the prophets as intermediaries, it was always Yahweh himself who took the initiative to relate to his people as a father and to hold them to the high standards of the covenant he made with Moses and their ancestors.

Despite the fact that Elijah had vanquished the prophets of Baal on Mt. Carmel, the struggle to eliminate Baalism was far from over. Queen Jezebel moved quickly to have Elijah arrested, hoping no doubt to reestablish the Baal cult by eliminating its principal opponent. Elijah, discouraged and confused over the prospect of having to continue a struggle which he thought had been concluded, fled for his life to Mt. Horeb.

There Yahweh appeared to Elijah in a gentle breeze (1 Kgs 19:13) to instruct him about the role he was to play in completing the victory which he had begun on Mt. Carmel. Elijah was to be an instrument in stirring up a revolution against the house of Omri so that the throne of Ahab and his pagan queen would be crushed forever. To assist Elijah in this endeavor, Yahweh was to give him a servant, Elisha ("God has saved"), whom Elijah was to anoint as his successor.

A Story of Yahweh's Justice

There is one more incident in the Elijah Cycle which we should consider. It concerns the story of Naboth's vineyard (1 Kgs 21).

68

Naboth's refusal to sell his vineyard to Ahab was based on Naboth's conservative interpretation of the tradition which held that Yahweh was the owner of the land given to the patriarchs and that those who held the land as descendants of the patriarchs were merely Yahweh's appointed stewards. Thus, Naboth's response in 21:3 does not mean that Naboth simply wanted to keep the land in his family. Rather, Naboth felt that he could not sell land which—through his ancestors—he held as Yahweh's trustee. The "elders and nobles" (21:8) were the leading men of the town who exercised the power of the king in their local province. After securing two false witnesses to accuse Naboth of blasphemy and treason (21:10)—both capital offenses—these city fathers stoned him to death. Evidently the property of one executed for a capital offense devolved upon the king. This would explain Jezebel's strategy and the ease with which Ahab took possession of the vineyard (21:15-16) after Naboth's death. Apparently Naboth's sons were executed at the same time (2 Kgs 9:26), further facilitating the transfer of ownership to Ahab.

Ahab's crime stirred Yahweh to action. He quickly instructed Elijah to condemn Ahab for his sins: the murder of Naboth *and* the usurpation of Naboth's Yahweh-given right to possess the vineyard. Again the real confrontation is between the Yahweh faith and Baalism—this time in the sphere of social justice. The convenant Yahweh had made with his people elevated king and commoner alike to a position of equality before the law. Baalism, on the other hand, tended to protect the interests of the wealthy, commerical classes in cities such as Tyre (Jezebel's homeland), where Baalism particularly flourished.

Therefore, in addition to the crime of murder, Ahab was guilty of perverting the tradition of social equality which had arisen from the Sinai Covenant (see p. 19). Yahweh, through Elijah, once again established his supremacy over Baal by condemning Ahab for his crimes and promising to wipe out his entire family. The actual execution of punishment was delayed because of Ahab's repentance (21:27-29). Ahab later died in a war against Syria (22:35), while his sons were executed at the hands of Jehu eight years later (see 2 Kgs 9—10).

THE COLLAPSE OF ISRAEL

The destruction of Ahab's family brings us into the Elisha Cycle, another source which D used, specifically in 2 Kgs 2:1—8:29. In 2 Kgs 8:7-15 we see that Yahweh used Elisha to bring about the final collapse of Ahab and the Omri dynasty by having Elisha select Hazael as king of Syria. This story once again illustrated that Yahweh's sovereignty extended even to the pagans. Yahweh used Hazael and the Syrians to punish the idolatrous Israelites by having them wage war against Israel in the last days of Ahab.

The fall of Omri's dynasty was facilitated first by Syrian aggression and then by the intrigues of Jehu, who murdered all of Ahab's heirs and established himself as king in Israel (841-814). During the five-king Jehu dynasty, Israel came to terms with Syria and enjoyed a temporary respite from foreign invasions, expanded its boundaries and increased its wealth. As we shall see in our next chapter, however, this outward pretense of calm and well-being was shot through with corruption and decadence. Baalism flourished, and acts of great injustice were perpetrated upon the poor by the rich. Because of Israel's cancerous condition, Yahweh once again raised up a pagan nation to chastise his people.

This time the instrument he used was the mighty Assyrian Empire, which had risen to dominance during the last two years of Israel's King Jeroboam II (783-743). In 721 B.C., led by their king Shalmaneser V, the Assyrians besieged Samaria, captured and destroyed it, and exiled nearly 30,000 of its leading citizens to the four corners of the Assyrian Empire. The northern kingdom of Israel was finished. It never again rose to power as an autonomous state, but henceforth was simply a vassal-state controlled by one pagan power after another. D's capsule teaching on the theological significance of the northern kingdom's tragic history appears in 2 Kgs 17:7-23. This passage is a classic statement of D's theology and should be read in its entirety before we take up the story of the fallen kingdom's southern neighbor, Judah

One final point to mention about the northern kingdom: The careers of Elijah and Elisha are two examples illustrating that fidelity to the Sinai Covenant had not completely died out in Israel. Another strong example of such fidelity during the very worst period of Israelite apostasy is the writing of the Elohist. Let us look briefly at the career of this northern writer and see how it relates to J's epic, which we considered in Chapter Six.

THE ELOHIST TRADITION

The Elohist ("E") lived in the northern kingdom and wrote from a northern perspective. As a result, his handling of the ancient Hebrew oral traditions differed in several respects from the southerner J's treatment of those same traditions. The most obvious difference between the two writers' approaches is seen in the name they used for God. E referred to God as *El*, or *Elohim*, while J preferred *Yahweh* for the name of God. *El*, in Hebrew, means simply "God"; while, as we saw in Chapter One, *Yahweh* has a much richer meaning, a meaning which was first revealed to Moses in the burning-bush theophany of Ex 3. The differing use of God's name tells us a lot about the approaches E and J took in composing their respective narratives.

J looked upon God as an almost human companion. Yahweh walked with Adam and Eve in the Garden of Eden "in the cool of the day" (Gn 3:8), and personally made clothes for the couple after their fall from grace. J has Yahweh constantly entering into his creatures' most mundane affairs, eager to relate on their level.

In Gn 18:1-15, for example, Yahweh comes to Abraham at Mamre and accepts Abraham's human hospitality. Yahweh promises Abraham that Sarah will have a son, and seems almost to get his feelings hurt when Sarah laughs at his promise. This is a very human picture of God, one which differed greatly from E's and which perhaps would even have offended E's sensibilities.

E's picture of God is a remote and awesome figure who speaks obliquely to people, using such means of communication as clouds, dreams and angels. For example, in Ex 19 when Moses goes up the mountain to receive the Ten Commandments, E says, "Moses spoke, and God answered him *with peals of thunder*" (19:19, emphasis added). In the very next verse, however, we have *J* telling us that "Yahweh *called* Moses to the top of the mountain" and "*said* to Moses..." (19:20, emphasis added).

One of the most famous of E's stories in Genesis, the testing of Abraham (Gn 22), would possibly have struck J as a rather negative presentation of how God related to humankind. God's instruction to Abraham to sacrifice his only son Isaac seems almost like a dirty trick to play on the old patriarch. Abraham had found it almost impossible to believe that he would ever have a son in the first place, and now God tells him to kill Isaac.

But there is method in E's madness. First of all, remember the social milieu in which E wrote. It was a society in which the foulest of pagan customs were practiced—including, at times, the *offering of human sacrifices*. King Ahab, for example, slaughtered his son Segub in sacrifice to Baal (1 Kgs 16:34). Perhaps it was the memory of Ahab's act which stirred E to write the story of Abraham's "sacrifice" of Isaac.

E was trying to demonstrate to his audience the difference

between El and Baal. El refused human sacrifice, while Baal relished it. Perhaps the only way E could drive this point home was to capture the reader's attention by placing the Isaac story in a setting which would have been familiar to them.

But E had another purpose in writing the Isaac story. Like J, E wanted to show that the God of his ancestors was a God in whom one could hope, even when all hope seemed lost. E, like J, wanted to encourage his readers to have faith in the promises God made to Abraham.

In concluding our brief account of the Elohist tradition, suffice it to say that E was writing to his audience just as J was writing to his. That is why, for example, E has Jacob tell his family in Gn 35:2, "Get rid of the foreign gods you have with you." E wanted his idolatrous northern brothers to understand that their father Israel had put all of his trust in the *one* God, and that they should do likewise.

The E tradition barely survived the collapse of Samaria in 721 B.C. Loyal and devout refugees from the fallen northern capital carried portions of E's epic south with them in their escape to Jerusalem. From that point on, the E epic was merged with the preexisting J epic, so much so that in some Pentateuch passages it is often very difficult to tell which verses are J's and which are E's. Because of this, scholars frequently refer to the merger of the J and E traditions as the "J-E epic tradition." In this J-E tradition, it is obvious that J's earlier narrative became predominant, while E's account receded into the background.

We still recognize, nevertheless, the independent significance of E's work, and we should be grateful to E for his contribution to the Pentateuch. Unlike J, who wrote in a time of great optimism and success, E wrote during some of the most depressing moments in Israel's religious history. It must have taken great personal courage to uphold the Sinai Covenant and the ancient belief in the one God when the official state religion often fostered the most decadent pagan polytheism.

When Samaria collapsed, the last vestiges of the loyal religious spirit which E had struggled to keep alive in Israel also collapsed. Not for centuries would pure devotion to the God of Abraham, Isaac and Jacob be seen again in the hill country of northern Palestine. If the covenant faith were to survive at all, it would have to do so in the south, in King David's royal city, on Mt. Zion,

the holy mountain, beautiful where it rises,
joy of the whole world.... (Ps 48:2)

Israel's hour had passed. Israel had failed to uphold the Sinai Covenant. Judah's time of testing had now arrived. The vital question of the moment in the minds of devout Judahite Yahwists was: Would Judah pass the test and remain faithful to Yahweh?

CHAPTER EIGHT

'HEAR, O ISRAEL!'

2 Kings, Deuteronomy

The test of fidelity to Yahweh was to come soon for Judah; the stage was set. In fact, one character in the drama looked very familiar: a member of the ruling family of the northern kingdom whose intrigues caught the kingdom of Judah in the same religious temptations Israel had faced.

There was one different factor in the south, however—the strong corps of priests who promoted pure Yahwism. The strength and resourcefulness of the Jerusalem priesthood was perhaps the main reason for the fidelity of several early Judahite kings. We see the influence of the priesthood in the story of Athaliah which is told in 2 Kgs 11.

Athaliah, the daughter of Ahab and Jezebel, made her entry into Judahite politics by marrying King Jehoram of Judah. When both her husband and her son died, Athaliah gained control of Judah's throne. Athaliah, as her mother Jezebel had done in Israel, promoted Baalism in Judah.

But this was Judah, not Israel. In Israel Elijah himself had not been able to drive Jezebel from her throne—at least, not without the assistance of Jehu's revolution, and this after Elijah's death. In Judah, however, no great prophet fomenting revolution was needed to overthrow Athaliah. The *priest* Jehoiada found a groundswell of popular support for his pro-Yahweh coup. The hated northern princess and her Baal entourage were eradicated; their altars and temples were destroyed.

HEZEKIAH AND JOSIAH—TWO LOYAL YAHWISTS

In spite of this example of Judah's loyalty to Yahweh during the time of Jehoiada, however, Judah soon started to go the way of the northern kingdom. By the time King Hezekiah reached the throne (716-687 B.C.), it was obvious to all that Judah had become as unfaithful to Yahweh as Israel had ever been. For that reason, Hezekiah—a loyal Yahwist—instituted a stern religious reform. D's praise of Hezekiah was lavish:

> He did what is pleasing to Yahweh, just as his ancestor David had done.... No king of Judah after him could be compared with him—nor any of those before him. He was devoted to Yahweh, never turning from him but keeping the commandments that Yahweh had laid down for Moses.
> (2 Kgs 18:3, 5-6)

Hezekiah reigned in Judah during perilous times. After the Assyrian forces had annihilated Israel, they began to invade Judah, striking down one city after another. By the year 701 B.C., the forces of the Assyrian King Sennacherib had reached the gates of Jerusalem. Would Jerusalem suffer the same fate as Samaria had 20 years before? The answer was uncertain. Hezekiah nearly lost his confidence and considered capitulating to Assyrian demands to surrender. But at the last moment, as had happened a century and a half before in the person of Elijah, Yahweh sent another of his prophets into action.

Isaiah of Jerusalem sent word to Hezekiah:

> "Yahweh says this: Do not be afraid of the words you have heard of the blasphemies the minions of the king of Assyria have uttered against me. I am going to put a spirit in him, and when he hears a rumor he will return to his own country, and in that country I will bring him down with the sword." (2 Kgs 19:6-7)

Hezekiah's response to Isaiah's encouraging word shows his strong faith in Yahweh. Unlike the northern kings, who during foreign attack fell so far from faith in Yahweh as to sacrifice their sons to Baal, Hezekiah sought Yahweh's guidance in the temple:

> "But now, Yahweh our God, save us from [Sennacherib's] hand, I pray you, and let all the kingdoms of the earth know that you alone are God, Yahweh." (2 Kgs 19:19)

Hezekiah's prayer was answered and, as events were soon to prove, Isaiah's prophecy was fulfilled. According to our D historian, the Assyrian army was struck down by an angel of Yahweh the night before its planned assault on Jerusalem, and Sennacherib returned home to be murdered by his sons (2 Kgs 19:35-37).

Unfortunately, Hezekiah's religious reform and his strong personal faith in Yahweh had no lasting effect on his people. After his death, Judah entered its darkest age under King Manasseh (687-642). What Jeroboam I was for the northern kingdom, our D historian assures us, Manasseh was for Judah—the apotheosis of evil. The reforms of Hezekiah were eradicated and Baalism reestablished. To enter into the spirit of the pagan revival, Manasseh burnt his own son in sacrifice.

After Manasseh's death, at the height of this time of utter betrayal of the Yahweh faith, the young king Josiah ascended to the throne. He would offer Judah its last chance to return to Yahweh.

The high point of Josiah's reign occured about the year 622 B.C and is recorded in 2 Kgs 22: Workers repairing the temple (perhaps tearing down Manasseh's pagan decorations) stumbled across a "Book of the Law." The high priest Hilkiah (father of the prophet Jeremiah) reported his find to Josiah who, as a faithful Yahwist, immediately sought the advice of the prophetess Huldah. Huldah's dramatic response appears in 2 Kgs 22:15-20. According to D, Josiah quickly moved to make this book the basis of his religious reformation. (It appears that in actuality Josiah's reform had already been underway for six years.) The characteristics of Josiah's reform are recorded in 2 Kgs 23:4-27.

What was this "Book of the Law," and what is its significance for our study of the Old Testament? The book stood for three basic propositions: (1) the condemnation of religious syncretism; (2) the establishment of Jerusalem as the central locus of worship in the land; and (3) the insistence upon Judah's absolute and total dedication to Yahweh. Since these three propositions are so strikingly similar to much of our present Book of Deuteronomy, it has been assumed by scholars that the Book of the Law was the *core source* underlying the final edition of Deuteronomy.

Deuteronomy means "second law" in Greek. This name was expressive of the belief that Israel failed to keep the "first law"—the one given to Moses on Mt. Sinai—and thus needed to try again with the "second law"—the one promoted by Josiah. Notice that in Dt 28:69 the editor says that the words of the covenant described in Deuteronomy are "*in addition to* the covenant" (emphasis added) Yahweh made with the people at Sinai. Let us take a closer look at this "second law" by considering the Book of Deuteronomy (Dt).

THE BOOK OF THE 'SECOND LAW'

It should be stated at the outset that not everyone is in agreement with D's account of the finding of the Book of the Law in the temple. Some scholars believe that the book was really "planted" in the temple, and that the story of its "discovery" was a clever scheme Hilkiah and Josiah cooked up to persuade people to accept the book's message. Even if that's the case, one can't really fault Josiah and Hilkiah for concocting a little drama to sell their program to the people. After all, the religious life of Judah had sunk to a very low level.

Whatever the truth concerning the finding of the Book of the Law, one thing is clear. This book, like the entire Old Testament which we are studying, did not magically take shape overnight. Rather, it was the product of several traditions going back in Judah to Hezekiah's time and back even further in Israel—receding into several centuries before the fall of Samaria.

Thus the Book of the Law and its descendant, our Book of Deuteronomy, were initially ancient *northern* products. Deuteronomy thus developed in the same environment that gave rise to the E tradition. That is why D and E share many of the same concerns and even use the same vocabulary. The northerners D and E, for example, refer to Mt. Sinai as *Mt. Horeb*, and they call the Canaanites *Amorites*. *Sinai* and *Canaanite* were southern expressions which J used in writing *his* epic.

The similarity between D and E does not end with their shared vocabulary. Both are almost obsessively concerned with the eradication and suppression of religious idols and images. Both are strict moralists, much stricter in many cases than J who, at times, seems almost easygoing in comparison.

Compare, for example, E's approach to Abraham's falsehood in Gn 20:1-13 with J's treatment of Isaac's lie in Gn 26:7-11. Consider D's insistence on the "ban" which we discussed in Chapter Three. The outlook of E and D must have been determined, at least partially, by the almost total collapse into apostasy which characterized their northern society. Because of their shock and disgust over what they saw going on all around them, they perhaps surmised that the only way to deal with religious syncretism was to take an absolute, "no-compromise" approach.

D's hard-nosed approach led to a view of foreigners quite different from the more sympathetic attitude of J. Although D stridently taught that Yahweh was God of the universe, he finds no place in Yahweh's plan for the salvation of Gentiles—contrary to J's belief that the descendants of Abraham had virtually a "mission" to the Gentiles. The only mission D wanted the Israelites to undertake to the Gentiles was to eradicate them root and branch! This, of course, may have been a teaching device D used to emphasize the danger of the Israelites' intermingling *religiously* with pagans. (D's tenderness at times shows through in spite of himself, as in Dt 10:19 where he admonishes his people to "love the stranger then, for you were strangers in the land of Egypt.")

The early D tradition, like E's epic, was carried by Israelite refugees fleeing to Jerusalem after the fall of Samaria in 721 B.C. Perhaps Hezekiah's religious reform developed out of his contact with northern Levites who brought the teaching of D into Hezekiah's court and into the Jerusalem temple. By the time of Josiah this teaching, like E's teaching, had been fairly well assimilated into the southern religion.

There is general agreement among scholars today that the older versions of this D tradition are preserved in Dt 5—26 and 28, while later traditions are evident in the other chapters of Deuteronomy. Since we have already discussed much of the teaching of Deuteronomy in previous chapters we will now focus only on its core teaching.

Essentially what is recounted in Deuteronomy is Moses' last speech to the desert Israelites* before they enter the Promised Land. Dt 1—4:40 is Moses' summation of the nation's glorious history to this point—glorious because it has been a history filled with Yahweh's mighty deeds and guided by his hand. Moses asked if anything like this was ever heard of before:

> "Did ever a people hear the voice of the living God speaking from the heart of fire, as you heard it, and remain alive? Has any god ventured to take to himself one nation from the midst of another by ordeals, signs, wonders, war with mighty hand and outstretched arm, by fearsome terrors—all this that Yahweh your God did for you before your eyes in Egypt?"
>
> (Dt 4:33-34)

Moses' "second address," Dt 4:41—11:32, is a summary of "the Law which Moses put before the sons of Israel" (4:44). A version of the Ten Commandments is presented (Dt 5:6-21), which differs only slightly from the version recorded in Ex 20:3-17. This serves to link the teaching of Deuteronomy with the classical Sinai tradition of Exodus.

---

*Here and following in this chapter *Israelites* and *Israel* are used in the original sense of the whole people.

New ground is then broken. Moses reminds the people that when they accepted him as mediator between themselves and Yahweh, they also accepted the responsibility to follow any laws which Yahweh would prescribe subsequent to the making of the Sinai Covenant. This statement leads to a discussion of these new laws—the "second law" we discussed earlier.

The new laws are set forth in Dt 6—26 and 28. As might be expected, considering what we have already learned about Deuteronomic theology, these laws deal with the following broad subjects: (1) the need for absolute fidelity to Yahweh in the new land, (2) the requirement of segregation from foreign neighbors and (3) the necessity of establishing one unique location in the land as the center of worship. Lesser laws and regulations, covering everything from feast days to tithing, are also listed.

This brief outline suggests that Deuteronomy concerns itself only with law and that D was merely a stuffy legalist, concerned with nothing more than "do's and don'ts." Such a picture of Deuteronomy and its author would be an erroneous one.

To correct that picture, turn to Dt 6:4-5 and read the "Great Shema'" (from the Hebrew word *shema'* meaning "hear"):

> "Hear, O Israel! The LORD is our God, the LORD alone! Therefore, you shall love the LORD, your God, with all your heart, and with all your soul, and with all your strength." (NAB)

This passage summarizes the *real* teaching of Deuteronomy. The basis of the nation's relationship with Yahweh was love, not law. Law served only to remind Israel of Yahweh's unconditional love. Law also served as the means of calling the people to return that love by requiring them to remain faithful to the covenant.

Thus we should not think of Deuteronomy as principally a legal code. Primarily, the book is a call to the nation to *hear (shema')*. "Wake up! Don't you remember," the author is pleading, "how Yahweh showed his *love* for you? Don't you remember how he took you out of Egypt, how he saved you from Pharaoh? How he brought you to the Promised Land?"

To his contemporary audience D's message is, "Look at you! Perverting Yahweh's gift of love by worshiping gods made of stone and clay and wood! If you don't wake up, if you don't *hear* pretty soon, Yahweh your God will return you to Egypt; he will put you back into slavery. *Shema'*, O Israel!"

Deuteronomy—the "second law"—was thus also a "second chance" for Yahweh's people. Once more—through the means of King

Josiah's reform—Yahweh would offer his covenant love to his people. Once more he would call them to be uniquely his own.

But time was running out; the people had to choose *now*. That is why the message in Deuteronomy is expressed with urgency. Words such as *now* and *today* recur frequently. In this magnificent recapitulation of the core of D's teaching, we see this sense of urgency expressed clearly:

> "See, today I set before you life and prosperity, death and disaster. If you obey the commandments of Yahweh your God that I enjoin on you today, if you love Yahweh your God and follow his ways, if you keep his commandments, his laws, his customs, you will live and increase, and Yahweh your God will bless you in the land which you are entering to make your own. But if your heart strays, if you refuse to listen, if you let yourself be drawn into worshiping other gods and serving them, I tell you today, you will most certainly perish.... I call heaven and earth to witness against you today: I set before you life or death, blessing or curse. Choose life, then, so that you and your descendants may live in the love of Yahweh your God...."(Dt 30:15-20)

JUDAH'S FINAL HOUR

Would the people of Judah "choose life"? That was the question of the moment during the reign of King Josiah. Josiah's reform did have some effect. Ironically, however, the very catalyst of this reform contained within itself a fatal flaw. That catalyst—D's teaching—was interpreted by some people in this fashion: "If we will be blessed when we follow Yahweh's law,.then *whenever* we find ourselves blessed, it must be an indication we are following Yahweh's law."

D's theology seemed to make an absolute equation between fidelity to Yahweh and prosperity, on the one hand, and between infidelity and disaster on the other. Real life, then and today, is much more complex. The good often suffer and the wicked frequently prosper. During the height of Josiah's reform, however, many people did believe that D's teaching promised them unassailable security.

During the height of Josiah's reign, Judah was free of foreign attack. Her enemies had problems of their own. Assyria was on the verge of being toppled by the Babylonians; thus Judah was free to run her own affairs. As a result, Judah prospered during the middle decades of Josiah's reign. This temporary prosperity lulled many Judahites into thinking Yahweh had found favor with them. They became complacent, impervious, as we shall see, to the warning of the prophets. Furthermore, their belief in the unconditional Davidic Covenant assured them that Jerusalem would never fall. Soon, very soon, this comfortable dream ended, and Judah's nightmare began.

In 609 Josiah was killed in battle. The Babylonians, who had supplanted the Assyrians as the dominant power of the day, then established themselves as the new tyrannical overlords of Palestine. Belief in D's teaching was soon shattered.

Under King Jehoiakim (609-598), religious syncretism was once again encouraged. The prophet Jeremiah went about proclaiming that Judah's days were numbered. The prophet advised King Zedekiah (598-587) to surrender to the Babylonian onslaught. Yahweh, Jeremiah said, would use the Babylonians to purge the people of their sins and lead them to a degree of fidelity to Yahweh which was impossible through purely human efforts. Zedekiah ignored Jeremiah's advice. He rebelled against the Babylonian king Nebuchadnezzar who, in retaliation, attacked Jerusalem, besieging it for 30 months (2 Kgs 25:1-3) until the inhabitants were worn down by famine.

In 587 B.C. Jerusalem, David's mountain fortress, fell to the Babylonians. There is perhaps no sadder scene in all the Old Testament than that of Zedekiah, the last descendant of the warrior-king David to rule in Judah, sneaking out of the city at night (2 Kgs 25:4), deserting its inhabitants to the cruel fortunes of war. Jeremiah (Jer 52:29) placed the number of those deported from the city to Babylon at 832. These were undoubtedly only the leading citizens. The *total* number of Judahites deported to Babylon (from the countryside as well as from the cities) in two waves of Babylonian deportation between the years 597 and 587 may have been as high as several thousand.

Thus ends the D history of Joshua/Kings, which we have been considering in these last six chapters. One of the greatest kidnappings in history had been completed. Practically the entire body of Yahweh's people had been carried off to foreign lands—the northern kingdom in 721 B.C. and the southern kingdom in 587 B.C.

We will continue our account of the life of Yahweh's people by taking up the story of Judah's half-century exile in Babylon in Chapter Eleven. But we must turn first to another subject. To understand both the period of the kings and the period which followed it, we must look more fully into a subject we introduced in Chapter Seven—prophecy.

CHAPTER NINE

'IT IS YAHWEH WHO SPEAKS'

Amos, Hosea, Isaiah, Micah, Zephaniah, Nahum, Habakkuk, Jeremiah, Ezekiel

Have you ever listened to a radio or TV evangelist preaching about the prophets? If so, perhaps you can remember a sermon that went something like this:

> "We see in the 39th chapter of the prophet Ezekiel that 'Gog' is soon going to invade Israel. Brothers and sisters, in this passage the prophet is speaking to us about Russia. As we see elsewhere, in Chapter 10 of the prophet Jeremiah, the 22nd verse, a 'mighty uproar' is 'coming from the land of the North.' What the prophet means by this is that Russia is also planning to invade the United States!"

This imagined preacher's interpretation of Old Testament prophecy is one that is common in some circles today. Proponents of this view define *prophet* as someone who lived long ago and had visions of a far-distant future. By some strange coincidence, that "far-distant future" always happens to be the very time when the person who holds to this definition of prophecy is living. Such people seem to think that the Old Testament prophets were isolated from all contact with their own historical environment and simply sat around coming up with oracles about the future.

Such an understanding of Old Testament prophecy is misinformed. The prophets of the Old Testament were totally absorbed in events of their *own* time. The words of the prophets were addressed to persons who lived in the same time and place as the prophets themselves. Thus, the prophet's vocation was not principally to predict the future, but to speak the word of Yahweh to the society in which the prophet lived.

It is true that there is a *timelessness* to the prophets' teaching. Because of this, we find a vast amount in the work of the prophets which *is* relevant to us today. But before we can consider the application of the prophetic message to *our* time, we must first understand the prophets' relevance to their *own* historical surroundings.

The origins of Old Testament prophecy may, in a sense, be traced back to Moses. The Hebrew word for prophet, *nabi*, basically connotes "one who speaks for God." According to that understanding of the word, Moses is the first *nabi* we encounter in the Bible. In Chapter Five we saw that Samuel, in addition to being a judge, was also considered a prophet. In Chapter Seven we considered the careers of Elijah and Elisha, two prophets who played a leading role in the politics of Israel in the ninth century B.C.

We now come to a consideration of the prophets whose names are associated with the traditional "prophetic books" of the Old Testament. This latter group was long ago given the name "literary prophets" because of their association with written books bearing their names. Another title which was frequently assigned to this latter group was "classical prophets," since it was assumed that these men established the criterion or model by which all future prophets were to be judged.

Who were these "literary," "classical" prophets, and how did they differ from their prophetic predecessors? Their names may be found in the table of contents of every Bible. In this chapter and the next we will be considering nine of these prophets: Amos, Hosea, Micah, Isaiah (1—39), Zephaniah, Nahum, Habakkuk, Jeremiah and Ezekiel. We will consider the rest of the prophets whose books are listed in the Old Testament in a later chapter when we reach the historical period in which a discussion of their careers will be more appropriate. For the next two chapters, our focus will be on the roughly two-and-one-quarter-century span bridging the gap between the start of Amos' career (c. 750 B.C.) and the last days of Ezekiel (c. 571 B.C.).

Aside from the obvious fact that the nine prophets named above are considered "writing prophets," what other differences do we find between them and their predecessors? To answer that question we must look more deeply into the history of prophecy.

Early Israelite prophecy had much in common with an ancient religious tradition that was pagan in origin. This tradition centered on the experience of the "seer" and the "ecstatic." Such persons had the ability to look into ordinary events and realities and draw out of them a supernatural meaning. As we saw in Chapter Five, Samuel was said to be a *seer*. The seer relied on dreams, visions and other altered states of consciousness to induce contact with the supernatural realm. Much like today's Hare Krishnas, who enter into meditative states through rhythmic dancing and chanting, the seers of old often used ritual dancing, chanting and other methods of bodily stimulation to bring on supernatural cognition. For that reason, *seer* and *ecstatic* were often synonymous terms.

By the time of Elijah, a different style of prophecy had begun to grow out of this earlier visionary tradition. We see this new approach reflected in the story of Naboth's vineyard, which we considered in Chapter Seven. In that scene we find Elijah concerned not so much with supernatural realities as he is with down-to-earth, practical realities. Elijah confronts King Ahab in the arena of day-to-day justice, and he does this—so far as we can tell—without ever having entered into a vision or trance. We find simply that "the word of Yahweh came to Elijah" (1 Kgs 21:17), without any description of *how* it came.

In other words, the emphasis in prophecy by Elijah's time had begun to shift from concern with the *methods* by which the prophet received Yahweh's word to concern with the *application* of that word to day-to-day moral affairs. We might say that prophecy in Elijah's time was becoming more relevant to the material realm and less confined to the supernatural realm. Like every generalization, that one is subject to qualification, but we do find in ninth-century prophecy a noticeable, growing emphasis on social justice.

With Amos, 100 years after Elijah, this prophetic concern with social justice explodes into maturity. With Amos we enter a new era of prophecy. In the eighth century the prophet is no longer an otherworldly visionary. He is instead a this-worldly spokesman for Yahweh, holding up to the sinful people their corruption, decadence and wickedness. The eighth-century prophet, far more than Elijah himself, enters right into the marketplace and shouts his message into the ears of people going about their daily affairs of buying, selling and trading. By Amos' time prophecy has come down to earth to become the principal vehicle for vexing and troubling the wicked, for shaking them out of their complacency and self-confident arrogance.

Old Testament prophecy thus established a bond between religion and morality which has been an essential constituent of the Judeo-Christian tradition ever since. No more could religion be separated from a concern with justice. Life's transcendent dimension, which religion preserved, could not be emphasized to the exclusion of life's material dimension.

Spiritual experience without moral discipline and concern for the welfare of others is a bogus religion, the eighth-century prophets taught. In particular, they said, this bogus religion is totally alien to the covenant which Yahweh long ago established with the Israelites in the desert. It was this Sinai Covenant, with its insistence on the worth and value of each Israelite before Yahweh, that was the inspiration for the prophets' mission.

Let us now look briefly at the careers of the nine men named above, locating them in their historical milieu and focusing on their concern for social justice.

SPOKESMEN FOR JUSTICE IN ISRAEL

Let us first consider Amos, the shepherd and dresser of sycamore trees from Tekoa in the southern kingdom. Called by Yahweh sometime during the reign of King Jeroboam II of Israel (783-743 B.C.), this country boy from Judah was sent to condemn publicly the sins of his polished, sophisticated northern neighbors. Instead of shrinking from the task, Amos poured out his denunciations with fervor. To the pampered rich ladies of Israelite high society he shouted out:

> Listen to this word, you cows of Bashan
> living in the mountain of Samaria,
> oppressing the needy, crushing the poor,
> saying to your husbands, "Bring us something to drink!"
> The Lord Yahweh swears this by his holiness:
> The days are coming to you now
> when you will be dragged out with hooks,
> the very last of you with prongs. (Am 4:1-2)

Amos' condemnations of the injustice in Israelite society (2:6-8; 5:10-12), his attacks on licentiousness and carnality (6:1-6), his denunciation of false piety and religious hyperactivity in the face of injustice (5:21-24) all went unheeded by the wealthy and the powerful.

Hosea, a contemporary of Amos, also denounced the evils of Israelite society. The Israelites had become little more than adulterers, Hosea said, by worshiping the Baals of the pagans, and by allowing pagan values to corrupt their society.

> [T]here is no fidelity, no tenderness,
> no knowledge of God in the country,
> only perjury and lies, slaughter, theft,
> adultery and violence, murder after murder. (Hos 4:2)

Like Amos, Hosea also predicted the destruction of the nation.

In 721 B.C., as we have seen, the Israelites were indeed "dragged out," as Amos had predicted, when the Assyrians under Sargon II crushed the northern kingdom, leveled the fine palaces of the wealthy to the ground and deported Israelite citizenry to the far-flung corners of the Assyrian empire. The northern kingdom of Israel was wiped from the face of the earth, never more to exist in ancient times as an independent state.

PROPHECY IN JUDAH

In Judah, several theories were advanced to explain the collapse of the northern kingdom. One of the more popular of these was the following: Yahweh's promise to keep David's throne secure forever (2 Sm 7) was an unconditional and irrevocable promise to David and his descendants. Thus those who were ruled by David's descendants— and only they—could benefit from Yahweh's promise. As a result, when Israel cut itself off from Judah in 931 B.C., it severed the relationship with the Davidic kings and set up kings who did not receive Yahweh's favor and protection.

This theory gradually led to the conviction that, since Judah *was* ruled by the Davidic line of kings, it could not possibly fall as Israel had. What proponents of this theory were really suggesting, perhaps without realizing it, was a state of affairs in which the obligations of the Sinai Covenant were no longer binding.

This theory was an abomination to two prophets who preached in Jerusalem toward the end of the eighth century and into the first two decades of the seventh century. Isaiah and Micah wanted to make it clear that their compatriots in Judah *were* fully bound by the obligations of the Sinai Covenant, and that in failing to carry out these obligations they were no better than those who had fallen in the north. Injustices perpetrated in Judah were just as foul as those committed by the northerners who had been chastised earlier by Amos and Hosea. And these injustices were just as likely to lead Judah to the same disaster as had befallen Israel:

> Woe to the legislators of infamous laws,
> to those who issue tyrannical decrees,
> who refuse justice to the unfortunate
> and cheat the poor among my people of their rights,
> who make widows their prey
> and rob the orphan.
> What will you do on the day of punishment,

when, from far off, destruction comes?
To whom will you run for help?
Where will you leave your riches? (Is 10:1-3)

To compound their evil, Judahites became all the more
"religious," fanatically dedicating themselves to piety and ritual. Their
outer lives were splendid and proper, while their inner lives were
corrupt and debased. That is why Micah so strongly attacked their
reliance on cultic ceremony to the exclusion of deeds of justice and
mercy:

—"With what gift shall I come into Yahweh's presence
and bow down before God on high?
Shall I come with holocausts,
with calves one year old?
Will he be pleased with rams by the thousand,
with libations of oil in torrents?
Must I give my first-born for what I have done wrong,
the fruit of my body for my own sin?"
—What is good has been explained to you, man;
this is what Yahweh asks of you:
only this, to act justly,
to love tenderly
and to walk humbly with your God. (Mi 6:6-8)

According to the D historian, Yahweh granted the southern
kingdom a reprieve because of King Hezekiah's stern religious reform.
At the 11th hour, when the capture of Jerusalem by the Assyrians
seemed certain, the devout Hezekiah pleaded with Yahweh to deliver
the nation.

That same night the angel of Yahweh went out and struck down a
hundred and eighty-five thousand men in the Assyrian camp. In the early
morning when it was time to get up, there they lay, so many corpses.
(2 Kgs 19:35)

Hezekiah died a year after the lifting of the Assyrian siege. As
we saw in the last chapter, his son Manasseh succeeded him and
reigned for 45 years (687-642), during which time he outstripped any of
his infamous predecessors in apostasy by wholeheartedly reestablishing
paganism in Judah (see p. 77). By the year 640 B.C., Judah was
languishing at death's door. Its religious spirit had been crushed and its
society was lacerated by the most flagrant injustices. It is during this
period that we begin to encounter another group of Yahweh's prophets.

Zephaniah, the first of this group, started his prophetic career during the last days of Manasseh. He gives us a vivid picture of the conditions in Judah at this time by describing life in Jerusalem:

> Trouble is coming to the rebellious, the defiled,
> the tyrannical city!
> She would never listen to the call,
> would never learn the lesson;
> she has never trusted in Yahweh,
> never drawn near to her God.
> The leaders she harbors
> are roaring lions,
> her judges, wolves at evening
> that have had nothing to gnaw that morning;
> her prophets are braggarts,
> they are impostors;
> her priests profane the holy things,
> they do violence to the Law. (Zep 3:1-4)

Faced with such degenerate conditions, Manasseh's successor, the loyal Yahwist King Josiah (640-609), took drastic measures to turn things around. As we saw in the last chapter, Josiah and his advisers instituted sweeping reforms, the chief of which involved exterminating all traces of paganism and establishing the temple in Jerusalem as the focal point of worship in Judah (see p. 77).

The basis of Josiah's Deuteronomic reform was a return to the Sinai Covenant. People who had for several generations come to think of the unconditional Davidic Covenant as the sole underpinning of their relationship with Yahweh were rudely jarred to hear priests and prophets calling them to return to the more ancient Sinai Covenant, which some Judahites had come to regard as something of a dead letter.

It seemed to some who were living during the first years of Josiah's reform that conditions were improving. Indeed, there were a few obvious signs of hope. The prophet Nahum joyously proclaimed the fall of Assyria, Judah's most dangerous foe, in the year 610 B.C.:

> See, over the mountains the messenger hurries!
> "Peace!" he proclaims.
> Judah, celebrate your feasts,
> carry out your vows,
> for Belial will never pass through you again;
> he is utterly annihilated. (Na 2:1,15)

It was soon realized, however, during the reign of King Jehoiakim (609-598 B.C.), that peace was not to be. When the Babylonians supplanted the Assyrians as even more vicious persecutors of Judah, people began to ask themselves why implementation of the Deuteronomic reform had not returned the nation to stability.

The writings of Habakkuk and Jeremiah provided an answer. Their prophecies showed that the Deuteronomic reform had not touched the inner lives of the people. It had been concerned only with externals. As Habakkuk asked Yahweh in prayer,

> Why do you set injustice before me,
> why do you look on where there is tyranny?
> Outrage and violence, this is all I see,
> all is contention, and discord flourishes. (Hb 1:3)

Jeremiah berated the "reformed" Judahites for supposing that, by concentrating on that part of the Deuteronomic reform which pertained to worship in the temple, they could ignore the underlying spirit of the Law, its basis in justice:

> "Steal, would you, murder, commit adultery, perjure yourselves, burn incense to Baal, follow alien gods that you do not know?—and then come presenting yourselves in this Temple that bears my name, saying: Now we are safe—safe to go on committing all these abominations! Do you take this Temple that bears my name for a robber's den? I, at any rate, am not blind—*it is Yahweh who speaks*." (Jer 7:9-11, emphasis added)

Jeremiah's words had little effect. His contemporary, a young man named Ezekiel, began to warn the people of Jerusalem that their city would soon be destroyed.

> "Near and far, they will scoff at you, the turbulent city with a tarnished name: where all the princes of Israel live, each one busy shedding blood, and a law to himself; where people despise their fathers and mothers; where they ill-treat the settler; where they oppress the widow and the orphan...where people take bribes for shedding blood; you charge usury and interest, you rob your neighbor by extortion, you forget all about me—*it is the Lord Yahweh who speaks*." (Ez 22:5-7, 12, emphasis added)

Jeremiah's sentiments were the same as Ezekiel's. He advised anyone who would listen to desert the city and surrender to the advancing Babylonian juggernaut—which, Jeremiah said, was the instrument Yahweh would use to chastise his people. In 587 B.C., the final blow came. Jerusalem was leveled to the ground, and her best citizens were deported to Babylon. According to one tradition, Ezekiel was carried off with the deportees. Jeremiah was not. Against his wishes he was instead taken by a band of refugees to Egypt, where he died.

CHAPTER TEN

'I WILL PLANT MY LAW WITHIN THEM'

**Amos, Hosea, Micah, Isaiah,
Jeremiah, Ezekiel**

You see the old man coming up the street, walking in the steady, relentless pace that marks the step of someone who has a mission to fulfill.

"He still walks the same way," you think. "Even though he's old now and limps slightly, he always walks as if he has some urgent business awaiting him at the end of his journey. What a strange man!"

You think back to another occasion. You were a child of seven or eight, part of a group of children that followed the man—younger and stronger then, broader of shoulder and quicker of step—to the temple area. He was striding boldly, heedless of your taunting.

"What are you going to do today, crazy man?" one of the children yelled as the others laughed. One boy threw pebbles at the man, who stood outside the temple silently gazing at the great stones that made up its wall.

"Yeah, what are you going to do today, crazy man?" another lad yelled out.

"Crazy man! Crazy man! Crazy man!" The children took up the chorus. Not knowing why, but afraid not to join in, you likewise began to yell and jeer at the man.

You remember how your parents had reacted to this odd character in those days, warning you not to talk to him or go near him. "He's a troublemaker!" your father had said. He told you how the man had rebuked the authorities, refused to listen to them, belittled them—and how the king had ordered the man arrested. "He's just trying to make a name for himself," your father scoffed. He says he's a prophet. Ha! He's no more a prophet than your Uncle Yeshua is!"

Your parents told how the man often made a public spectacle of himself, appearing in the streets in a loincloth or wearing a yoke on his shoulders. They had watched him one day, shrieking to the crowds at the gate of the temple, "Do you think that vows and consecrated meat can free you from guilt? How can you boldly say, 'We have wisdom! We have the Law!'? You have turned this temple into a robbers' den!" (See Jer 11:15, 8:8, 7:11).

Your parents had watched in derision and disgust. Finally your mother urged your father, "Do something!" He and some others dragged the man from the temple area. "We'll give you a good beating the next time you show up, crazy man!" they shouted. "See that you stay away from God's house with that kind of talk!"

In your memories, the taunts of the adults blend with the mimicry of the children—"Crazy man! Crazy man!" You see him again, facing the temple walls, seeming not to notice the taunts of the children, or at least not to mind. He was used to this kind of treatment now; perhaps he even expected it. After staring silently at the temple, he spoke in a low monotone. There was deep pain, tiredness, frustration in his voice:

> You have seduced me, Yahweh, and I have let myself be seduced;
> you have overpowered me: you were the stronger.
> I am a daily laughing-stock,
> everybody's butt.
> Each time I speak the word, I have to howl
> and proclaim: "Violence and ruin!"
> The word of Yahweh has meant for me
> insult, derision, all day long. (Jer 20:7-8)

Several of the children snickered, but gradually you and the others drifted away. For some reason it was no longer fun to ridicule the man.

Today, over 15 years later, a lot of people have changed their opinions about the man. You are one of them. You feel ashamed of the way you and your friends ridiculed him years ago.

"Maybe he's not so crazy after all," you've heard people say.

It's not the same Jerusalem it was in your youth. People are afraid. There's no security anymore, no stability. The priests seem so confused! And the king—first one alliance and then another! The army is corrupt and seems powerless to stop the Babylonians.

As the old prophet comes nearer you decide to take a chance.

You rush up to talk to him. Perhaps he won't remember how you and your friends have mistreated him all these years. Perhaps he'll have an answer to your questions.

"Sir!" you shout. "Please, sir. May we talk?"

The old man stops and turns toward you. Those serious, penetrating eyes that you used to call "crazy" seem to burn right through you. Yet you feel accepted by the old man, almost as if you had found a friend for whom you had been searching for some time. You feel a sense of peace, of serenity. You feel free to approach him. His old face has many lines etched into it by years of pain. Yet he looks at you and smiles a leathery old smile.

"Come, my friend," he says. "Walk with me to Yahweh's house. We must still try to teach them. There may still be time."

CHRONOS AND KAIROS

The previous chapter's brief and condensed introduction to the social justice teachings of the nine preexilic prophets could lead to a distorted understanding of prophecy. The preexilic prophets were not concerned only with social justice. It would be erroneous to imagine them as frenetic social workers trying to eliminate poverty or to picture them as liberal do-gooders calling for some sort of Marxist utopia.

As I tried to show in the descriptive scene that opened this chapter, the prophets were first and foremost *men of God*. Their concern for the welfare of the poor and downtrodden grew out of their own *deeply spiritual* experience of Yahweh's presence in their lives. They were in a sense Yahweh's "alter egos."

They spoke up for the poor and the abused, not because they had some pet sociological theory to advance, but because they sensed in the very depths of their beings the *pain* which the poor suffered at the hands of their oppressors. Like Yahweh, they were motivated not by social principle, but by an empathy bred of a deep and abiding *love* for their brothers and sisters. This love flowed freely from the Sinai Covenant, and the prophets wept when the terms of that covenant were abrogated by king, priest and false prophet.

That is why the prophets condemned social injustice. They recapitulated in their innermost sensibilities the shock and disbelief which Yahweh himself experienced as he saw his beloved people perverting the free gift of love which he had given them on Mt. Sinai. The prophets ached inwardly as Yahweh ached. "Why do you turn away from me, my people? What is it I have done to you? Don't you know how I *love* you, how I want you to be my very special possession? Yet, if you must persist in your infidelity, I must correct your ways. I will bring you back to me through the means of this catastrophe which you are bringing upon yourself." This was Yahweh's message through the prophets—his co-sympathizers, his fellow sufferers, his empathetic spokesmen who experienced deeply how Yahweh felt when his people betrayed him at every turn.

When we enter the prophetic world, we enter into a different form of time. Our English word *time* does not express the depth of the prophetic experience. To improve our perception, it is helpful to turn to the Greek conception of time, summarized not in one word, but two: *chronos* and *kairos*.

Chronos is our ordinary understanding of time. One event follows another. Day follows day into infinity. We could call this conception "horizontal time."

Kairos, on the other hand, is "vertical time." It is not a perception of the flow of events in sequence but a perception of the infinite depth of *each* moment of time. It is the "timeless time" of the poet and the mystic who perceive in a sudden deep intuition the unity of all time. "The entire universe is contained in a grain of sand," according to an old Hindu saying; in *kairos* all moments are condensed into one.

This sense of *kairos* is alien to our culture, where we seldom live in the present moment. We "rational modern-day people" spend most of our time either brooding about the past or awaiting the future.

The Old Testament prophets were unlike us in this respect. They *were* able to enter fully into the present: They lived much of their lives in *kairos*, while at the same time being firmly established in *chronos*; they perceived what was *universal* about their particular environments. For that reason, the prophets are highly relevant to us today. Their depth of vision offers us many insights into our own condition—the universal human condition, especially as it concerns our own relationship with Yahweh.

THE CLASSICAL PROPHETS

It is helpful to keep this deeper understanding of time in mind as we read the prophetic books of the Old Testament. The prophetic books are less concerned with *chronos* than the other Old Testament books we have previously considered. In Joshua, Judges, Samuel and Kings, we were presented with an ordinary chronology in which event followed event and past preceded future. In the prophetic literature we leave behind this orderly chronology and enter into *kairos*.

The prophets are not so much concerned with the *sequence* of events as they are with the inner *meaning* of events. Thus, we often find in the prophetic literature *no* orderly presentation. To our modern minds this is jolting and confusing.

As we shall see, the prophetic materials are often arranged not in a *logical* order but in an order that constantly reinforces the deeper significance of the prophetic message. That is why we can be reading at one minute about the utter destruction and havoc Yahweh will soon bring upon his people and in the next find a description of Yahweh's eternal love, protection and promise to *restore* his people to perpetual peace and security. To the prophets such contrasting elements did not produce discord, because both elements were part of the same underlying truth embodied in Yahweh's deep love for his people.

We should also keep in mind that not every passage we read in a prophetic book was actually written by the prophet whose name appears in the title. The core teachings of the various prophets were preserved, summarized, enhanced and expanded by later editors who wanted to insert their own message between the lines of that core teaching. Each prophetic book of the Old Testament is a complex mixture of teachings—some written by the actual prophet and some inserted by a later editor who unabashedly used the prophet's name to promote his *own* teaching.

It would take a lengthy and tedious volume to straighten out which verses in a particular book are the "very words" of a particular prophet and which are later insertions. What we will do here is simply summarize some essential themes from the original works of the prophets we are considering, without analyzing those passages which have come down to us from later editors.

Amos

Let us start again with Amos. We have considered (see pp. 86-87) his concern for social justice, how he condemned the rich

> because they trample on the heads of ordinary people
> and push the poor out of their path.... (Am 2:7)

Let us look briefly at another message of Amos, a theme which he began but which would become more fully developed by later prophets. This theme concerns the notion of the "remnant." Amos was harsh and extreme in his denunciation of the sins of the Israelites; his prediction of impending doom seemed to allow no possibility for hope for the condemned Israelites. Yet, there is a mysterious passage in

Amos which seems to suggest the possibility of Yahweh's future restoration of fallen Samaria:

> Like a shepherd rescuing a couple of legs or a bit of an ear
> from the lion's mouth,
> so will these sons of Israel
> be rescued, who now loll in Samaria
> on the corner pillows of their divans. (Am 3:12)

This brief and solitary suggestion by Amos that Yahweh's chastisement of his sinful people would not be total, that a "bit" of his people would survive, was developed more fully by Amos' successors. As we shall see particularly in Isaiah's teaching, this notion of "the remnant" who would survive to keep Yahweh's promises alive was to become a mainstay of Israel's hope in its continued existence as a people.

Hosea

Amos' contemporary, Hosea, was much less of an extremist in his approach to prophecy than Amos. Whereas Amos came in like a steamroller, crushing everything in his path, Hosea tactfully appealed to the sinful Israelites' emotions. Hosea held up to the people a picture of Yahweh's steadfast love for them, hoping that by doing this he would stir the Israelites to repentance.

To vivify this image, Hosea compared the Israelites' conduct to adultery. Yahweh had betrothed his people in the desert, Hosea said, and they had responded not by covenant love, but by infidelity and debauchery. As a result, to bring his people back to him, Yahweh had to take corrective action. Through the prophet, Yahweh said of Israel,

> ...I am going to block her way with thorns,
> and wall her in so that she cannot find her way....
> Then she will say, "I will go back to my first husband,
> I was happier then than I am today." (Hos 2:8, 9b)

Hosea's own life was a reflection of the pain which Israel's adultery had caused Yahweh. Yahweh had told Hosea to marry the prostitute Gomer, who proved to be as faithless to Hosea as Israel had been to Yahweh. (We find in this incident the beginnings of a teaching method which later prophets would use. Instead of merely preaching to the people, the prophets would frequently perform symbolic actions which would drive home their message more dramatically than mere oratory. We find this to be especially true in the careers of Isaiah, Jeremiah and Ezekiel.)

Hosea held out to Gomer the possibility of repentance and return to lawful wedlock. In the same way, Yahweh kept open to the very end the possibility of reconciliation with his people, if only they would repent:

> Israel, come back to Yahweh your God....
> Provide yourself with words
> and come back to Yahweh.
> Say to him, "Take all iniquity away
> so that we may have happiness again
> and offer you our words of praise...." (Hos 14:2-3)

Micah

As we have seen, Israel spurned Yahweh's offer. When the northern capital was leveled to the ground in 721 B.C., Yahweh's hope for renewal of the covenant relationship with his people focused on Judah. The southern prophets whom Yahweh appointed rose to the occasion, urging the Judahites to repent of their apostasy and return to Yahweh.

The southern prophet Micah, who spoke out for justice in Judah, stresses another important theme which we should consider. Micah was particularly harsh when it came to denouncing Judah's wicked *leaders*. False prophets, corrupt priests and idolatrous kings were all leading the people down the road to disaster.

Yahweh would not allow this situation to go on forever, according to Micah. He would not break his promise to keep David's throne secure in perpetuity. Yahweh would raise up a leader for his people who would be an ideal Davidic ruler—a *true* shepherd who

> ...will stand and feed his flock
> with the power of Yahweh,
> with the majesty of the name of his God.
> They will live secure, for from then on he will extend his power
> to the ends of the land.
> He himself will be peace. (Mi 5:3-4a)

It is obvious here that Micah is not thinking of just any king, but of an ideal Davidic ruler who would fulfill in his person David's virtues of loyalty, fidelity and love of Yahweh. We see here the first stirrings of the concept of the "messiah" (from the Hebrew *masiah*— "anointed"). In its fully developed form in late Judaism, the notion of messiah would be applied to an unknown descendant of David who would bring salvation to the Jews and extend Yahweh's sovereignty to all peoples. The messiah's reign would thus be absolute and universal.

Isaiah of Jerusalem

Micah's contemporary, Isaiah, would develop this nascent messianism more fully. According to Isaiah, the name of the messiah would be

Wonder-Counselor, Mighty-God,
Eternal-Father, Prince-of-Peace. (Is 9:16)

The messiah's rule would usher in "a peace that has no end" (9:6). He would be possessed of

a spirit of wisdom and insight,
a spirit of counsel and power,
a spirit of knowledge and of the fear of Yahweh. (Is 11:2)

He would rule with equity, giving "a verdict for the poor of the land" (11:4).

The question everyone wants answered, of course, is: Whom did Isaiah foresee as this messiah, and when would he begin his reign?

To answer that question, we must keep in mind once again the prophets' talent for functioning simultaneously in the spheres of *chronos* and *kairos*. Maybe Isaiah was looking forward to an ordinary political ruler—perhaps Hezekiah—who would institute a return to pure Yahwism in Judah. This interpretation of Isaiah's prophecy is not contradicted by the text. Much of the language quoted above is similar to standard royal investiture ceremonies during which Judah's kings were showered with lavish and exaggerated praise. This might be compared to the "honeymoon period" following the inauguration of a new American president, in which only good things are said about the new leader during his first few weeks of office.

But there is a deeper dimension to Isaiah's prophecy that is equally obvious from a reading of these messianic passages. While Isaiah undoubtedly hoped for an ordinary political ruler who would come to the throne and quickly reestablish righteousness in Judah, he also had a vision of a greater type of king who would somehow reign in perpetuity. The reign established by this ideal king would be universal and perfect. Isaiah himself doubtless lacked real understanding of how his prophecy was to be fulfilled. Nevertheless, it is clear that he foresaw the coming of this king with absolute certainty.

Thus, if we look at Isaiah's messianic writings from the perspective of *chronos* we find one meaning. If we enter with the prophet into *kairos*, we find a much deeper, fuller meaning. It is this deeper meaning of the messianic passages in Isaiah which was accepted by the early Christian Church when it applied these passages to Jesus of Nazareth, acclaimed as "the Christ" (the "Anointed").

The message of hope found in Isaiah's messianic prophecies was mirrored in his teaching on the remnant. Isaiah foresaw a day when Judah would be restored, a day when a faithful few would continue the mission of Yahweh's fallen people:

> "The surviving remnant of the House of Judah shall bring forth
> new roots below and fruits above.
> For a remnant shall go out from Jerusalem,
> and survivors from Mount Zion.
> The jealous love of Yahweh Sabaoth will accomplish this...."
> (Is 37:31-32)

The establishment of the remnant, like the inauguration of the messiah's rule, would be solely Yahweh's doing. Yahweh's interest, both in preserving the remnant and in raising up the messiah, would be based on his continuing desire to make his people holy, as he himself was holy. Isaiah constantly stressed the holiness of Yahweh, especially as it contrasted with the wickedness of the people. It was Yahweh's holiness which impelled Yahweh to purge his people of their guilt. Like Isaiah himself, who was cleansed of impurity on receiving the prophetic call from Yahweh, and cried out,

> "Holy, holy, holy is Yahweh Sabaoth.
> His glory fills the whole earth." (Is 6:3)

The entire people would have to be purged of their sins and remade into a holy people.

Jeremiah and Ezekiel

As we have seen, during the height of Isaiah's career, in 701 B.C., Judah was granted a temporary respite from foreign attack when the Assyrian siege of Jerusalem was lifted. Many Judahites grossly misinterpreted this event as a sign of the unconditional security which Yahweh would grant those who lived under the rule of Davidic kings. It was this complacent and self-righteous attitude which so irritated the last two prophets who preached in preexilic Judah. Jeremiah and Ezekiel excoriated the people of Judah for their arrogance and self-assurance in the face of impending doom. Through Jeremiah the Word of Yahweh shattered the people's illusion of security:

> "...Peace! Peace! they say,
> but there is no peace.

They should be ashamed of their abominable deeds.
But not they! They feel no shame,
they have forgotten how to blush.
And so as others fall, they too shall fall;
they shall be thrown down when I come to deal with them
—says Yahweh." (Jer 8:11-12)

Ezekiel likewise disrupted the people's pleasant dreams of comfort and security. To the people who laid plans for a comfortable future, who asked, "Shall we not soon be building houses?" (Ez 11:3), Ezekiel spoke Yahweh's bitter message:

"I shall drive you from the city and hand you over to foreigners...I shall execute justice on you; and so you will learn that I am Yahweh...."
(Ez 11:9, 10)

With the careers of Jeremiah and Ezekiel, we reach the high point of Old Testament prophecy. Except for the prophet known as "Second-Isaiah," prophecy was to take on a new dimension after the Exile—to such a degree that much of what is later called "prophecy" is actually a genre distinct from the writings of the men we have considered in *this* chapter.

Jeremiah, priest and prophet from Anathoth, son of the Hilkiah who discovered the Book of the Law in 622 B.C., is a man about whom we know a great deal. Ezekiel, on the other hand, is something of a mystery. We know that Jeremiah began his prophetic career in Judah sometime during the reign of King Josiah, no sooner than 627 B.C. and perhaps as late as 609 B.C. As for the date and location of Ezekiel's ministry, there is a great deal of debate.

Some scholars think Ezekiel was taken to Babylon in 597 B.C. with the first wave of deportees and that all or most of his oracles originated from Babylon. Other scholars think that he was "exiled" only to a Judean village outside of Jerusalem in 597 and that he didn't reach Babylon until 587, after the final collapse of the kingdom. The intricate debate accompanying these opposing positions need not occupy us here. We will consider Jeremiah and Ezekiel together, not because we know with certainty that they simultaneously occupied the same geographical location, but because they developed two important Old Testament themes in much the same way in their writings.

As we have seen, both Jeremiah and Ezekiel were firmly planted in the classical prophetic tradition begun by Amos. Both condemned sinful Judah for its apostasy; both promised Yahweh's swift and terrible judgment on the nation. Similar to the vocation Yahweh had given his earlier prophets, he called Jeremiah

"to tear up and knock down,
to destroy and to overthrow...." (Jer 1:10)

And to Ezekiel, Yahweh said,

"Son of man, say, 'The Lord Yahweh says this to the land of Israel:
Finished!...Now all is over with you; I mean to unleash my anger on you,
and judge you as your conduct deserves and force you to answer for all
your filthy practices.'" (Ez 7:2-3)

In this respect, then, the careers of Jeremiah and Ezekiel are a
continuation of the vocations of the prophets who went before them.

A NEW COVENANT

We find, however, a new prophetic teaching in both Jeremiah
and Ezekiel, something hinted at in earlier prophecy but now fully
stated. It is the development of this new message which was one day to
guide Yahweh's people from reliance on D's preexilic theology toward
reliance on a radically *new* theology.

This new teaching would also eventually lead the people of God
from the Old Testament to the New, from knowledge of the old
covenant to an awareness of the infinite horizons of a new covenant.
This new covenant would prove once and for all the unlimited measure
of love which Yahweh offered to his people.

We have seen how the predominant theology of the last years of
Judah was the D teaching underlying King Josiah's reform.
Superimposed on this theology was the promise of 2 Sm 7 that David's
throne would remain secure forever.

We have also seen how both the teaching of D and the Davidic
promise were abused by many people in Judah during its last days. On
the one hand, people believed that by strictly observing the external
requirements of the Deuteronomic Code they would *earn* Yahweh's
constant protection. On the other hand, they believed that the
unconditional nature of Yahweh's promise to David in 2 Sm 7
absolutely *guaranteed* the safety of the nation. These attitudes were
based on a fatal misunderstanding of the relationship to which Yahweh
had called his people.

The central teaching of the Exodus event had been Yahweh's
free election of this people as his very own. Nothing they did then and
nothing they could do now would *merit* Yahweh's election. Like all
true gifts, Yahweh's choosing of the Israelites was the outgrowth of
Yahweh's deep and *steadfast love* for them. What Yahweh wanted

from his people in return was the free response of faithful love. The whole purpose of the Sinai Commandments and the later Deuteronomic Code was to instruct Yahweh's people in the ways of a loving people.

Yet they weren't able to get the message. Not even after he sent the prophets to them, not even after Hosea pleaded with them to turn from their adulterous ways and come back to Yahweh their true husband, could the people understand that, first and foremost, Yahweh called his people to a relationship based on love.

Since neither the spirit of the Sinai Commandments nor the Deuteronomic Code had been strictly honored by the people, Yahweh had to find a new way to bind his people to himself in love and fidelity. What would he do? Would Yahweh start all over again with another covenant? The answer was yes and no.

Yahweh would make a new covenant with his fallen people, but this time it would be a covenant that he himself would observe *for* his people. He would not give them a covenant like the old ones he had made, which seemed doomed to failure from the outset because of his people's inherent weakness and sinfulness. Through Jeremiah, Yahweh described the terms of this amazing new covenant that he had in mind:

> See, the days are coming—it is Yahweh who speaks—when I will make a new covenant with the House of Israel (and the House of Judah), but not a covenant like the covenant I made with their ancestors on the day I took them by the hand to bring them out of the land of Egypt. They broke that covenant of mine, so I had to show them who was master. It is Yahweh who speaks. No, this is the covenant I will make with the House of Israel when those days arrive—it is Yahweh who speaks. Deep within them I will plant my Law, writing it on their hearts. Then I will be their God and they shall be my people. There will be no further need for neighbor to try to teach neighbor, or brother to say to brother, "Learn to know Yahweh!" No, they will all know me, the least no less than the greatest—it is Yahweh who speaks—since I will forgive their iniquity and never call their sin to mind. (Jer 31:31-35)

These verses stress that Yahweh's new covenant would be preserved, not by anything the people themselves did, but by Yahweh's own activity at work deep within the recesses of each human heart. The fulfillment of this new covenant would not depend on human effort. Its preservation would be somehow assured by Yahweh himself, who would plant within each person the seeds of its fulfillment. Yahweh's people would thus finally come to learn that their salvation was based not on any concept of human merit, but solely on their gratuitous and loving election by Yahweh.

Like Jeremiah, Ezekiel also foresaw a radically new

development taking place in the Yahweh-Israel relationship. From the harsh denunciations of his preexilic prophecies, Ezekiel turned to a message of hope and consolation. Yahweh's punishment of his people was necessary to bring them back to a proper relationship with him. After a brief period of purgation, however, Yahweh would do something new in the life of his people:

> "...I am going to take you from among the nations and gather you together from all the foreign countries, and bring you home to your own land....I shall give you a new heart, and put a new spirit in you; I shall remove the heart of stone from your bodies and give you a heart of flesh instead. I shall put my spirit in you, and make you keep my laws and sincerely respect my observances." (Ez 36:24, 26-27)

Like Jeremiah, Ezekiel taught that the success of this new relationship between Yahweh and the people would not be based on anything the people merited:

> "And so, say to the House of Israel '...I am not doing this for your sake, House of Israel, but for the sake of my holy name, which you have profaned among the nations where you have gone. I mean to display the holiness of my great name....And the nations will learn that I am Yahweh—it is the Lord Yahweh who speaks—when I display my holiness for your sake before their eyes.'" (36:22-23)

With Jeremiah and Ezekiel a new day had dawned. Marvelous new wonders lay ahead. Yahweh's promises through these two prophets outstripped any promises he had ever made before. Yahweh's relationship with his people now promised to be more *intimate* than anything the people had experienced before. Mysteriously, Yahweh would dwell *within* them—his law written on their hearts, his spirit alive within their souls!

No doubt these great promises—uttered by Jeremiah and Ezekiel from the deep perspective of *kairos*—were not understood or appreciated by the defeated and dispirited exiles in Babylon. It would take years, centuries even, before the Jews understood the full significance of these marvelous words. For now, there were more practical matters to consider. How, for example, were the exiles to relate to their foreign captors? Were they to take root in Babylon and grow? Or were they simply to wait for Yahweh to return them to their homeland?

With broken hearts and crushed spirits, the exiles surveyed their new surroundings—the fine palaces, gardens and temples of Babylon—and wondered: "Can Yahweh truly be Lord of the universe? Has he perhaps forgotten all his promises? What will the future bring? Do we descendants of Abraham even *have* a future?"

CHAPTER ELEVEN

'THE LIGHT OF THE NATIONS'

Ezekiel, Leviticus, Genesis, Exodus, Isaiah

Miriam was an old woman now. She had first entered the magnificent city of Babylon seated on her mother's knee, bouncing along on the old donkey which her father had yanked and tugged all the way from Jerusalem. Her brother had tried to keep their small flock of goats together on the long trip. Along the way the family had to eat two of them.

All in all Nebuchadnezzar's soldiers had not been bad to the people in Miriam's party. She remembered one rough, smelly old infantryman who used to smile at her and teach her games. Forty-nine years ago as she reckoned it. Forty-nine years! What changes she had seen come over her family and her friends!

The worst part of those first days was the absence of the temple. The first time she ever saw her father cry occurred in those first few weeks in Babylon.

"How can we live without our temple?" he had moaned, sobbing as he hugged Miriam's mother. "What will become of us? Has God forgotten us?"

Many of her people adapted well to the new land. Miriam's friend Sarah told her one day, "My father has gotten a good position in a market. But the Babylonians there made him swear an oath to their god Marduk. He felt bad about it at first, but he says we'll all get used to it after a while."

That night, Miriam told her father what Sarah had said.

"Will you look for work like Sarah's father?" she asked him.

Her father took her gently by the arms and looked into her eyes.

"No, Miriam. We are Yahweh's children. Our ancestors were Abraham, Isaac and Jacob. We will not work for the Babylonians. We will not live among them. One day we will go back home. You will live to see it, I promise you."

Miriam's father died that next spring. Miriam thought he had been very sad the last weeks of his life. The day before his death, he told Miriam again, "We will go back home one day, Miriam. You will live to see it."

Miriam never forgot her father's words. Through the long years in Babylon she encouraged her friends, her new husband Jonathan and, eventually, her three children never to forget that one day they would return to their homeland.

Her oldest, Simon, was just like her father, Miriam thought. He loved Miriam's stories about the temple and the old days in Jerusalem. Simon began studies with the group of elders who had established a school in the city. They admired Simon's practical wisdom. An old priest took Simon under his wing and taught him the ancient ways. The old man showed Simon his collection of scrolls.

"These are very precious, Simon," he said, "We must organize these words and write their message down for our people so that our traditions do not get lost."

Simon met many elders and priests in the school. One man in particular fascinated Simon. He was so fresh and positive. He constantly talked about returning to Jerusalem. Simon loved to tell Miriam at night what this man had said to the students.

"Mother, this man says Yahweh is about to rebuild Jerusalem. He says the Lord Yahweh is about to deliver us from captivity."

"Listen to this man, Simon," Miriam said. "Tell me often what he says."

One day, some weeks later, Miriam awoke to hear her neighbors buzzing about in the street. Simon was at school. Miriam's old friend Leah was screeching at the top of her lungs, instructing her grandson how to pack her cooking pots safely.

"Isn't it wonderful, Miriam?" Leah asked. "We're all going home. You and I, Miriam, we know where home is. Isn't it wonderful?"

Miriam simply stared at the scene. Suddenly Simon came through the door, tears running down his face.

"O Mother! Isn't it marvelous? Yahweh has answered our prayers. We're going home, Mother, to Jerusalem, to our holy city. I will see the temple! Aren't you happy, Mother?"

Miriam sat down softly and whispered. "Yes, Father, we will go home! We will return! I will live to see it!"

TOWARD A POSTEXILIC FAITH

In this chapter we begin the story of the Jews and Judaism, the people and the faith which came into existence in Babylon and grew to maturity after the return of the exiles to conquered Judah. Neither the Jews nor Judaism, of course, were created from nothing. They were products, respectively, of the people and the faith which had been formed centuries before in the Sinai desert.

Our word *Jew* comes from the Hebrew word *Yehudi*. It simply means one who is descended from the preexilic Judahites. Continuity exists, therefore, between the descendants of Abraham before and after the Exile—continuity in more than name. While the Jews in Babylon had brought with them from Judah very little in the way of material goods, they had brought a priceless treasure of religious tradition. It was from this ancient tradition that a new kind of Jewish faith was to be fashioned.

The exiles themselves probably had little intuition that an old age had passed and a new age was coming to birth. On the contrary, most Jews in Babylon at the start of the Exile probably believed that, once Yahweh returned them to Judah, things would start over just as before. In particular they thought Yahweh would reestablish the Davidic kingship and would, they hoped, return them to the type of life-style that characterized Solomon's reign.

Were the good old days of David and Solomon gone forever? As we shall see, a major thrust of much of the biblical literature we shall consider in this chapter is the promise of a glorious new day for defeated Israel. (In this chapter we return to using *Israel* to refer to *all* of the descendants of Abraham, not just to the northern tribes.)

The focus in this chapter and in Chapter Twelve will be the period beginning with the Babylonian Exile and ending with Alexander the Great's rise to power. This two-and-one-half-century period spans the nearly 50 years spent in exile, the return to Judah, the rebuilding of the temple and the walls of Jerusalem, and the renewal of the people's covenant relationship with Yahweh.

In this period the exiles benefited from the work of creative religious thinkers and teachers who were able to reshape and redefine the themes of Israel's sacred tradition, thus laying the foundation for the "new" Jewish religion. They gave hope to the exiles, bolstering their faith in Yahweh. When the people were at last permitted to return

107

to Jerusalem, where they faced problems similar to their ancestors, there were prophetic voices to encourage and warn, urging the people not to repeat the very mistakes which had led to their banishment to Babylon.

In this chapter we will look at two themes which were to become an integral part of Jewish religious thought in the aftermath of the Exile: the holiness of Yahweh—and his people; and the universality of Yahweh as compared with the more narrow view of preexilic faith. And we will meet two creative geniuses of this period—both of whom had great influence on this reshaping process and yet remain shrouded in anonymity: the P writer/editor (actually a whole school of thought) and the prophet known to us as "Second-Isaiah."

EMPHASIZING YAHWEH'S HOLINESS

One of the major themes of postexilic Jewish thought was the *holiness* of Yahweh. Because Yahweh was holy, the people were to be holy. This "sanctifying" activity naturally led to a stress on the "priestly" function within the religion of Israel.

From King to Priest

A hint of this characteristic appears in the writings of Ezekiel, the prophet whose teaching spanned the period leading from the old Judah to the new. In Ez 40—48 we are given the prophet's vision of the restored nation, a nation which Ezekiel himself never lived to see.

In these chapters we find no description of a political entity similar to the monarchical state of preexilic Judah. Instead of referring to the ruler of the restored nation as "king," Ezekiel in his prophecies constantly refers to him as "prince." By doing this he suggests that kingship in the restored nation would be of lesser significance than previously. And indeed kings *would* be of lesser significance. Ezekiel foresaw a nation governed not by political rulers but by religious leaders—by priests and Levites—and this was precisely what happened in the period of Judah's restoration.

Ezekiel's interest in the priestly function grew out of his concern for holiness. For Ezekiel, Yahweh's principal characteristic was his awesome, transcendent holiness; and Yahweh's greatest purpose was to make his people holy as he himself was holy. This concern for sanctification could not really occupy the interests of a political ruler such as a king. Rather, *sanctification*—making holy—is traditionally associated in *all* religions with the function of the priest. And with Ezekiel, Israel's religion began to be shaped into a priestly religion.

Belief in the Davidic Covenant did not die out during the restoration period. Neither did hope for the coming of a messiah pass away. Yet the Davidic Covenant and messianism—both of which could only be fulfilled in the person of a king—would be given a new interpretation by the biblical writers of exilic and postexilic Judaism.

'Holiness Code'—An Introduction to P

Earlier (see Chapter Two) we discussed the P source—the Priestly school of biblical writing. Since we are now dealing with the time period in which this school was active, we will turn our attention to its concerns—especially the themes of holiness and, in a moment, Yahweh's universality.

P's stress on holiness is so similar to Ezekiel's that some scholars consider Ezekiel the founder of the P school. This is debatable; what is evident is that both used ancient Israelite sources which had long before stressed the importance of holiness in Israelite religion. P's work with a great deal of this ancient material has been integrated into our present Book of Leviticus (Lv).

One particular ancient source appears in Lv 17:1—26:46, a unit designated by scholars as the "Holiness Code." To get a taste of P's handling of the holiness tradition in the Book of Leviticus, let us look at one excerpt from the Holiness Code—Lv 19:1-18.

The overriding preoccupation of P in this passage is to stress that Yahweh is a holy God and that his people must consequently be a holy people. The Hebrew *qòdes* (*holy thing, holiness*) connotes "separation" or "distancing." That which is holy is opposed by its very nature to that which is profane or debased. The gap between the profane and the holy can be bridged only through some ritual of purification (examples of which abound in Leviticus) and by the all-holy Yahweh transforming his creation into a condition of holiness.

In choosing his people Israel from all the peoples of the earth, Yahweh has begun the process of transforming his people into this state of holiness. Yet there is still work for his people to do: They must cooperate in Yahweh's sanctification process by behaving as if they are indeed holy. Moral choices are thus very significant.

The moral imperatives listed in Lv 19:1-18 are aids to assist Yahweh's people to become truly holy, but the emphasis remains always on Yahweh as the source of all holiness. (Notice the repetition of "I am Yahweh" after each set of commands.) Humanity unaided cannot be holy. Israel is to be holy *because Yahweh is holy* (see 19:2).

Notice also that holiness, while transcendent and an attribute of Yahweh alone, comes to human beings only in a social setting. Human beings become holy by serving the needs of their brothers and sisters. The famous proclamation of Lv 19:18, "You must love your neighbor as yourself," did not in P's time apply to *non*-Israelites. Nevertheless it demonstrated the strong connection in P's thinking between holiness and justice.

The P tradition did not stand only for ritual and cultic sacrifice—as we could very well be tempted to think while plowing through the gory and tedious chapters of Leviticus. As with the D tradition before it, the P school looked upon the externals of religious practice as a means to a higher end—namely, strengthening the love relationship between Yahweh and his people.

While we may have outgrown the primitive means stressed in Leviticus for relating to Yahweh, we cannot overstate the importance of P's concern for ritual and sacrifice in the overall development of the Jewish and, later, the Christian religion.

THE UNIVERSALITY OF YAHWEH

The narrow confines of the preexilic faith had been shattered by the exiles' experience in Babylon. A new perspective on Yahweh's saving actions was developing out of that painful fragmentation. For Judaism to survive in a strange land, its religious writers would have to show how it was that Yahweh's power encompassed *all* the earth.

P skillfully captures this new thrust. In several examples—two parts of P's creation account in Genesis, P's handling of the Abrahamic covenant, and the Passover story—we will sample how the P school was able to encompass a development in Israel's understanding of Yahweh while continuing to root this reshaped faith in the age-old traditions of sacrifice and ritual.

'In the Beginning...'

While Leviticus is *entirely* P's work, it is by no means the only book in the Old Testament to which P contributed. As general editor of the Pentateuch and contributing editor to many other preexilic books, P inserted his teaching into virtually every Old Testament book we have so far considered with the exception of the prophetic literature. We have seen in earlier chapters examples of P's writing in Exodus and Numbers. P also made a major contribution to Genesis. In fact, P is responsible for putting Genesis into the form we have today. He took the Old J-E epic which was carried by the exiles to Babylon, and while in Babylon began to put on his finishing touches.

P begins his Genesis account "in the beginning" (Gn 1:1). P

exceeds even J in scope by carrying Yahweh's work of creation back to the beginning of time. Living in the midst of the pagan Babylonian culture, P wanted his exiled audience to understand that Yahweh alone is God of the universe, not the Babylonian deities. Yahweh created the entire world and thus controlled all events and all earthly powers—even the mighty Babylonian empire.

P's creation account (Gn 1:1—2:4a) is by no means "scientific." That is to say, P was a theologian, not a scientist, and wrote his creation story with only a rudimentary concern for the details of *how* Yahweh created the universe. Obviously, P's awareness of physics, astronomy and cosmology was very primitive. We can't expect him to have had the scientific knowledge of an Einstein or a Newton. What little he knew about science was erroneous, judging by present scientific knowledge. For example, he believed with other ancient peoples that the sky was a great vault which supported a huge body of water above it (Gn 2:6-8).

Since P was a theologian and not a scientist, it is fallacious to insist that P's creation account is "literally true." Nevertheless, there is no conflict between P's creation account and modern scientific evidence indicating an evolutionary development of matter. That is because P's principal purpose was not to teach *how* Yahweh created the universe, but *that* he created it. If P were alive today he would be perplexed by the argument between creationists and evolutionists.

For P, Yahweh's mighty creative power was at work in the universe from the very first moment of time—whether that first moment was millions of years ago or in the year 4,004 B.C. as biblical literalists insist. If P were writing today he would feel very comfortable saying, "A million light years from earth, Yahweh induced the first thermonuclear explosion, and the light from that explosion traveled through the vast reaches of space to shine on earth for the first time." P wanted to stress that Yahweh was creator and Lord of the universe. The *means* Yahweh used to manifest his creative power would not have been something on which P would have rigidly insisted.

Creation of Man and Woman

From a general discussion of P's methodology in Genesis, let's center in briefly now on some further examples of his work there and in another book of the Pentateuch, Exodus.

Let us look first at P's account of the creation of the human race in Gn 1:26—2:3. We see in 1:26 that, as a result of resemblance to God, humans share one of God's prerogatives—dominion over the other living creatures of the earth. The Hebrew word for *subdue*—

kabas—suggests "trample under foot." P makes it clear, however, that in exercising dominion over God's other creatures and subduing the earth, men and women act only at God's behest. Thus that work must ever reflect the respect which God himself had for his own creation, a creation found to be "very good" (1:31). The "paradise motif" suggested in 1:29-30, in which humans and animals live in harmony, represents P's attempt to assimilate his own material into the Yahwist's paradise narrative. Both P and J thus emphasize the blissful existence enjoyed before the fall.

The phrase "Let *us* make" (1:26) has generated much commentary. The generally accepted viewpoint among scholars is that: (1) no hint of a trinitarian God is implied by P, (2) P does not suggest the notion of God's consultation with heavenly consorts. Rather, the plural is used either to suggest (3) absolute fullness—that God is so complete in himself that his decision-making *alone* is like that of a group of people deciding to act; or (4) it is a rhetorical device by which any individual would deliberate about a projected course of action—as we might say, "Let's do it," meaning simply, "I'll do it."

In speaking of humanity's creation in the image of God, P is not implying a *physical* copying of the transcendent God. Rather, this likeness to God lies in *reflective consciousness:* Human beings possess self-awareness, the quality which is most "god-like" about God.

We see P's concern for the sabbath in his account of God's rest from his labors (2:2). *Rested* (Hebrew, *shabath)* could perhaps better be rendered "desisted." God did not need to rest. He stopped work simply because all of creation was "completed" (2:1). Although P obviously had his own interests to promote by having God obey the sabbath, he was not simply writing the Priestly law about keeping the sabbath into the creation story. Rather, P was trying to show that it is in human nature to rest from labor every seventh day. All humans, not just Israelites, are here being urged by P to heed God's own example.

Abraham, Father of Many Nations

The second Priestly passage we will consider is Gn 17:3-9. Here P gives his account of one of several ancient Israelite covenant traditions. P no doubt drew his account, at least partially, from the same source that inspired the Yahwist in Gn 15—the unconditional Davidic Covenant tradition of 2 Sm 7:16.

The emphasis in P's covenant account, as in the Davidic Covenant, is on *perpetuity.* God's pact with Abraham and his descendants is everlasting (17:7). The *Jerusalem Bible* translation—"a Covenant in perpetuity" (Gn 17:7)—suggests better the solemnity of

God's promise and its legally binding effect, an emphasis which would have been significant to the Jews of P's time. For the exiles living in Babylon, it would have taken great faith to believe that God truly intended to honor his promise to Abraham. This passage should thus be read as P's attempt to encourage the faith of his fellow Jewish exiles.

The change of names from Abram to Abraham (17:5) is significant. Probably the two words were originally simply variant spellings of the same name. The change, however, from *Abram* (Hebrew: "the father is exalted") to Abr*a*ham ("father of a host of nations") more vividly explains the new title which God gives to the aged patriarch: (*of nations* in Hebrew is *ab hamon*).

The name change is thus God's way of legitimizing the elevated status he gives to Abraham and to his progeny.

Note P's universal emphasis: Abraham is to be father not just of Israelites, but of non-Israelites as well. As the early Christian Church was to interpret the passage, Abraham became the father of all who believe, regardless of their nationality.

The Passover
Our third example of Priestly writing comes from the chapter on the Passover, Ex 12. The Passover was an ancient Israelite feast whose origins probably predate the Exodus. The Israelites likely adapted it from a Semitic ritual regularly practiced by the indigenous peoples they encountered in Canaan. The description in 12:11 reflects a ritual originally celebrated by nomads and shepherds to assure the fertility of crops and the fecundity of flocks. The Israelites absorbed the ritual into their own religious institutions, rid it of its pagan elements and made it a solemn feast day.

As P develops the passage, he is careful to detail the exact *liturgical* elements which each Jewish family was to follow in recreating the feast each year. The time referred to, "tenth day of this month...fourteenth day" (12:3, 6), would be the time of the lunar calendar's month when the moon would be fullest—an ideal time for nomads to travel by night.

The etymology of *Passover* (Hebrew: *pesah*) is disputed. It probably stems from the Hebrew verb *psh*—"to jump"—which suggests Yahweh's action as described in 12:13: He "jumped over" each Hebrew dwelling that was appropriately marked.

We have seen in these examples from P's writing the emphasis which exilic Judaism placed on the universal applicability of Yahweh's actions. P blended the new with the old, pointing the way for Judaism to follow on the eve of its return to its ancient homeland.

SECOND-ISAIAH: PROPHECY DURING THE EXILE

P was not the only creative genius at work among the Jews exiled in Babylon. Another great writer, a prophet, also contributed to the developing Jewish religious consciousness. No one knows this prophet's true name. Scholars have given him the nickname "Second-Isaiah" based on the fact that his works are included with the writings of Isaiah of Jerusalem, whom we considered in the last chapter. Is 40—55 certainly belong to this exiled prophet, while *parts* of Is 56—66 come from both Second-Isaiah and a later writer called "Third-Isaiah."

Lumping together three different writers under the name of one man may strike us as somewhat bizarre. But to the Jews who put the Old Testament together, it made a great deal of sense. If there were room left over on a scroll containing the entire works of one writer, what could be more economical than to fill in the leftover space with verses from another writer! Remember that paper was nonexistent in those days; every effort had to be made to preserve the few papyri and other writing materials that were available. In the case of the three "Isaiahs," there was also a certain inherent logic in putting the works together, since some of the same themes were common to all three.

We saw that Isaiah of Jerusalem had denounced the seventh-century Judahites for their infidelity to Yahweh and warned of their impending punishment. He also prophesied that a remnant, purged by Yahweh of its sins, would return to Judah in triumph. Second-Isaiah, writing 150 years after his namesake, prophesied to the exiles that *they* were Yahweh's chosen remnant, and that their deliverance from bondage was imminent. Second-Isaiah's message is thus one of consolation, optimism and hope.

Like P, Second-Isaiah wanted to establish for his exiled audience the universal supremacy of Yahweh. Also like P, he wanted to emphasize Yahweh as universal creator. In majestic language that outstripped even P's universalism, he wanted to show that Yahweh was Savior-God to all peoples.

Let us now examine the motivation of this great prophet and poet and see the message he wanted to give his fellow exiles.

Second-Isaiah was inspired to write by the world-changing events which took place in the Babylonian empire in the fifth decade of the Exile (549-539 B.C.). During this time a new power arose to threaten Babylon's mastery of the ancient world. As the Babylonians had once supplanted the Assyrians, now the Persians superseded the Babylonians as the chief power among the nations. In 539 B.C. Cyrus the Great of

Persia won a significant battle against the Babylonians, breaking the will of the Babylonian leadership to resist further the shifting tide of power. As a result, the city of Babylon surrendered easily to Cyrus; its inhabitants even greeted him as a liberating hero.

Unlike the Assyrians and Babylonians, Cyrus decided to pursue a policy of religious toleration. He encouraged conquered peoples to maintain their own religious traditions (unless, of course, this led to political self-assertiveness). Consistent with his policy, Cyrus issued a decree of liberation for the Jews living in exile, encouraging them to return to Judah and rebuild their temple. He even ordered the natives in Palestine who had occupied the exiles' former homeland to help pay for this project!

It was against the background of Cyrus' magnanimity and protection that Second-Isaiah wrote. To the gloomy exiles who had perhaps begun to think they would stay in Babylon forever, Second-Isaiah cried out,

> Shout for joy, you heavens, for Yahweh has been at work!
> Shout aloud, you earth below!
> Shout for joy, you mountains,
> and you, forest and all your trees!
> For Yahweh has redeemed Jacob
> and displayed his glory in Israel. (Is 44:23)

Second-Isaiah compared Yahweh's liberation of his people from Babylon to the original Exodus event, when Yahweh had led his people from Egypt to the Promised Land. Unlike the first Exodus, which terminated eventually in the catastrophe of the Exile, this new liberation would lead to the final and permanent establishment of Yahweh as universal sovereign and of his people as the dominant power on earth. Speaking through the prophet to his defeated and discouraged people, Yahweh promised:

> With you I will make an everlasting covenant
> out of the favors promised to David.
> See, I have made of you a witness to the peoples,
> a leader and master of the nations.
> See, you will summon a nation you never knew,
> those unknown will come hurrying to you,
> for the sake of Yahweh your God,
> of the Holy One of Israel who will glorify you. (Is 55:3b-5)

Second-Isaiah thus reasserted the messianic prophecies begun by Isaiah of Jerusalem, but again with a new twist. Second-Isaiah foresaw the *entire people*, the chosen remnant, as fulfilling many of the messianic prophecies. He thus felt that the nation in some dramatic way would assert the prerogatives of the Davidic messiah foreseen by earlier prophets. The messianic era was about to begin, he believed, and the remnant returning to Judah would play a major role in ushering in this new age.

But how would the people do this? Further, what were to be the characteristics of the remnant's mastery over the nations? Were the people to dominate the nations—as foreign empires had done—or were they to serve in some other capacity in carrying out Yahweh's plan?

The answer to these questions is found in Second-Isaiah's most famous poems—the Songs of the Suffering Servant. These four songs are located in the following chapters and verses of Second-Isaiah: (1) 42:1-9; (2) 49:1-6; (3) 50:4-11; and (4) 52:13—53:12.

In the first song, we find that Yahweh speaks of his "servant" as one who is endowed with Yahweh's spirit. The servant will be the

> ...light of the nations,
> to open the eyes of the blind,
> to free captives from prison,
> and those who live in darkness from the dungeon. (Is 42:6-8)

The natural question to ask is, "Who is this servant?" In the second song we learn more about the servant's identity. In 49:3 we are told specifically that the servant is "Israel." Paradoxically, in 49:5-6, we find that the servant will "gather Israel to him" and "restore the tribes of Jacob and bring back the survivors of Israel." Is the servant one person or the whole people?

In the third servant song, the servant speaks, revealing more about his identity.

> The Lord Yahweh has given me
> a disciple's tongue.
> So that I may know how to reply to the wearied
> he provides me with speech.
> Each morning he wakes me to hear,
> to listen like a disciple.
> The Lord Yahweh has opened my ear. (Is 50:4-5)

This third song rather clearly affirms that the servant is thought of as an individual. He reveals that he will have to undergo much suffering on behalf of the people.

The full measure of the servant's suffering is set forth in the final song. The servant will become

"a thing despised and rejected by men,
a man of sorrows and familiar with suffering,
a man to make people screen their faces;
he was despised and we took no account of him." (Is 53:3)

The fourth song also reveals *why* it is that the servant will suffer:

"...[H]e was pierced through for *our* faults, crushed for *our* sins.
On him lies a punishment that brings *us* peace,
and through his wounds *we* are healed." (Is 53:5, emphasis added)

By the end of the fourth servant song we might conclude that Second-Isaiah had entirely shifted his emphasis from the servant as people to the servant as one person. Yet, this would be to look upon Second-Isaiah's prophecies from our own perspective, not his.

Through the four servant songs, Second-Isaiah was describing principally the Jewish mission to the nations. The Jews would be Yahweh's servant. They would be a light to the nations and would establish justice for all peoples. In doing this, they would have to suffer. Through suffering they would bring healing and liberation to others. Second-Isaiah thus saw the servant primarily as a collective entity, representing the entire Jewish community.

Second-Isaiah was principally concerned with the redemptive suffering which the people as a whole would have to endure in bringing the non-Jewish nations to salvation. He used the theme of the servant as individual in the same way that the word *Israel* itself was used in Genesis and later books to refer both to the man Israel (Jacob) and the people whom the man fathered. Second-Isaiah was not, therefore, suggesting a dichotomy between an individual and the community when he described the servant. His main teaching was that Yahweh would lead the exiled remnant back to Judah and give them a mission to bring all peoples under Yahweh's lordship. In doing this, the Jews would have to endure much suffering.

Second-Isaiah's theology is thus much more mature and realistic than the D theology which we considered earlier. D clearly equated suffering with wickedness and blessing with righteousness. Second-Isaiah probed deeper into the ways of Yahweh and, in contrast to D, taught that Yahweh's chosen ones may very often have to suffer for the sake of righteousness. This deeper reflection on Yahweh's ways marks Second-Isaiah as one of the Old Testament's most creative and original thinkers.

This brief overview of the exilic authors P and Second-Isaiah enables us to turn now to Jewish history during the period of the restoration.

CHAPTER TWELVE

'REJOICE, DAUGHTER ZION!'

1 and 2 Chronicles, Ezra, Nehemiah,
Malachi, Zechariah, Obadiah, Joel

Our knowledge of the two-century period beginning with the Jews' return to their homeland in 538 B.C. is very incomplete. Nevertheless, we have been left an historical record which preserves a broad outline of Jewish life during this period: the First Book of Chronicles (1 Chr), the Second Book of Chronicles (2 Chr), Ezra (Ezr) and Nehemiah (Neh). In addition much supplemental information is provided in the writings of the prophets Haggai, Zechariah, Malachi, Obadiah and Joel. In this chapter we will be discussing the teaching preserved for us in these books.

Having terminated the D history which we followed from the Book of Joshua through the Second Book of Kings, we must now take up the writings of a new historian named by scholars "the Chronicler." The Chronicler wrote his history probably sometime in the mid-300's B.C., shortly before the Greeks began to rise to power in the ancient Near East. Like all biblical books, the Chronicler's narrative underwent later revisions and, as we now have it, contains material dating from perhaps as late as 200 B.C.

When we say "the Chronicler's work," we mean 1 and 2 Chronicles, Ezra and Nehemiah. Like the D historian, the Chronicler used preexisting sources to compile his history. In 1 and 2 Chronicles his chief source was the D history itself. Thus, 1 and 2 Chronicles essentially retells the story of kingship in Israel, beginning with David and ending with the fall of Jerusalem. In Ezra and Nehemiah, the Chronicler continues his account down to about the year 400 B.C.

1 AND 2 CHRONICLES: A SPECIAL SLANT

Since we rather exhaustively covered the history of the northern and southern kingdoms in Chapter Five through Eight, we will not repeat that here. Let us simply note the general difference in perspective between the books of Samuel and Kings on the one hand and 1 and 2 Chronicles on the other.

The first section (1 Chr 1:1—9:34) sets forth Israel's family tree, beginning with Adam and continuing down to the names of the first exiles who returned to Judah. The Chronicler's purpose in tracing the roots of the returning exiles is to establish continuity with the past. He wants to show that the Jews resettling conquered Judah are firmly in line with the ancient traditions, and thus firmly established in Yahweh's plan. The most prominent place on the Chronicler's family tree is occupied by the tribes of Judah (David's tribe) and Levi. That is because the Chronicler centers his theology on David and the Levites. It is thought that the Chronicler was himself a Levite, perhaps a cantor or a doorkeeper in the restored temple.

Pro-David

According to the Chronicler, King David was more of a religious leader than a political leader. The thrust of David's reign (1 Chr 9:35—29:30) was to establish the temple cult and to organize the liturgy, music, worship and the various duties performed by temple functionaries. One scholar has counted 323 verses in 1 and 2 Chronicles devoted to concerns of David's temple, as opposed to only 77 verses in the books of Samuel.

This is a clear indication of the Chronicler's viewpoint. He saw David's reign as centered on the temple and its cult. Military and political concerns are glossed over in comparison to the history presented in 1 and 2 Samuel. In particular, anything casting David in a negative light is entirely omitted (e.g., his affair with Bathsheba, his days as a Philistine mercenary). As the Chronicler remembers it, the early days of the Israelite monarchy were absorbed in worship, praise and liturgy. And the leaders of this religious state (after the king) were the Levites.

Pro-Levite

The Chronicler shows a definite pro-Levite bias in his writing. This contrasts to P, who emphasized in Exodus and Numbers that the priests were the leaders of the Israelite worshiping community and that the Levites were their assistants. The Chronicler, while not downplaying the importance of the priests' function in offering the temple sacrifice, emphasizes the equal importance of the Levites in their duties: leading the temple singing, keeping the temple secure from intruders, maintaining the treasury and, especially, teaching and interpreting the Law.

Anti-Samaritan

After a brief description of Solomon's reign (2 Chr 1:1—9:31), the Chronicler finishes off 2 Chronicles by surveying the acts of good and bad kings in Judah from Rehoboam (931) to Zedekiah (587). Unlike the Deuteronomic historian, the Chronicler ignores the reigns of the northern kings. To the Chronicler David's role in reestablishing the temple cult completely eclipsed the doings of the apostate northerners. In addition, like most of his contemporaries in fourth-century Judah, the Chronicler probably despised the "Samaritans," as the descendants of the northern kingdom were called in his time.

When the Jews returned from Babylon, the Samaritans— regarded by the Jews as a mongrel people because of their mixed blood—had asserted a right to share in the restored temple cult. The Jews rebuffed the Samaritans on this issue, and the latter responded by harassing the Jews as they attempted to rebuild the temple and walls of Jerusalem. By the Chronicler's time, about 200 years after these incidents, open hatred existed between Jew and Samaritan. The Chronicler thus scrupulously avoided any reference in his history to the Samaritans' preexilic ancestry.

The Chronicler's theological conclusion about the fall of the kingdom in 587 differs in one important respect from D's conclusion. D saw Judah's destruction and the Exile as the result of the accumulated sins of the entire people over a period of 400 years. The Chronicler, however, believed in individual, not collective, responsibility and blamed the ultimate fall of Jerusalem only on its last king, Zedekiah. The Chronicler had absorbed this idea from Ezekiel, who had taught this new theory of responsibility for sin two centuries before (Ez 18).

With the conclusion of 1 and 2 Chronicles, the Chronicler moves into the history of the restoration proper. We now take up the account of that history in the books of Ezra and Nehemiah—and supplement it with outside historical data.

THE EXILES COME HOME

The exiles first began to return to Judah in 538 B.C. under the governance of Sheshbazzar, a descendant of David who is not called king, but "high commissioner" (Ezr 5:14). Sheshbazzar fades out quickly in the chronicle and is replaced by Zerubbabel, who led another wave of exiles back to Judah in 521 B.C.

Sheshbazzar and Zerubbabel are mysterious figures. They both simply disappear from the story after their brief tenures of governance are mentioned. It is clear that neither man ever became king of Judah, even though a great deal of messianic expectation surrounded the leadership of Zerubbabel. The prophet Zechariah, for example, writing between 520 and 518 B.C., called Zerubbabel the "Branch" (Zec 3:8), meaning that as Zerubbabel's reign developed Judah—like a replanted branch—would begin to grow into a tree, the symbol for her future supremacy over the nations in messianic times:

> "On that day, says the LORD of hosts, you will invite
> one another under your vines and fig trees." (Zec 3:10, NAB)

Despite Zechariah's messianic prophecies, the leadership of Judah passed to the high priest Joshua. Never again was Judah to be governed by a king; henceforth, priests were to rule the Jewish state. This state of affairs required a drastic overhaul of Jewish messianic thinking. With no king on whom to pin their messianic hopes, prophets more and more envisioned a different kind of king who would fulfill Yahweh's promise to the House of David.

Between the tenures of Sheshbazzar and Zerubbabel (537-521) initial work on the temple stopped, partially due to harassment from the Samaritans and other local people who feared a Jewish political and religious revival. The cessation of work was also caused, however, by the Jews' absorption in more worldly affairs—such as rebuilding their homes and reestablishing economic ties with non-Jews. At this point the prophets Haggai and Zechariah began their respective missions, urging their compatriots to put first things first by quickly completing the temple reconstruction.

Spurred on by these prophets and encouraged by renewed promises of Persian protection from King Darius I (522-486 B.C.), the Jews recommenced construction and finished the temple in 515 B.C. The contrast between the lowliness of this second temple and the magnificence of Solomon's temple can be assessed from the statement in Ezr 3:12 that old-timers who had known the first temple in its heyday wept aloud at the sight of its shabby replacement.

Nevertheless, Yahweh's people had come home and true worship of Yahweh could begin anew. Yahweh's holy, priestly people were ready once again formally to renew their love relationship with their God. Unlike in former times, that relationship was now to center exclusively on the temple, the priesthood and the teaching of the Levites. The prophetic spirit so prominent in preexilic times began to diminish in importance. Concern for the Law and cult gradually became supreme in Judah.

The days of king, kingdom and prophet were gone. The era of priest, Levite, temple and, especially, concern for the Law was beginning. To see how this occurred we must take up the Chronicler's account of the careers of Ezra and Nehemiah.

EZRA THE PRIEST, NEHEMIAH THE GOVERNOR

One of the most intriguing scholarly debates about the Old Testament arises from the question, "Who arrived in Jerusalem first, Ezra or Nehemiah?" Ezra, the priest, left Babylon to minister to the *religious* needs of the repatriated Jews, while Nehemiah, appointed governor of Judah by the Persian king, provided *political* leadership to his fellow Jews.

This debate need not occupy us save to note that the Chronicler's purpose in placing the Book of Ezra before the Book of Nehemiah in his narrative is to show that in terms of *theological significance*, the reestablishment of the temple cult was prior in *importance* to the rebuilding of the walls of the city. The Chronicler undoubtedly has his chronology mixed up on this detail as well as on others, but that is relatively insignificant. The Chronicler's purpose was not to leave behind a scientific history, but a record of the important religious happenings of the time as they touched on the reestablishment of the temple.

One of the central events of Ezra's ministry was the promulgation of the "Book of the Law of Moses" (Neh 8), which represented the establishment of the Pentateuch as the founding document of Judaism. Since it was due to Ezra's efforts that the Pentateuch was first established as the Jews' national religious book, Ezra is often called "the father of Judaism." Henceforth, the Pentateuch and, gradually, the other Old Testament books (collectively called "The Prophets") would be collected, edited, taught and disseminated among Jews everywhere.

Notice in Neh 8:7 that during the first reading of the Book of the Law, the "Levites explained the Law to the people." The Levites' responsibility as teachers and interpreters of the Law was to expand greatly after the time of Ezra and Nehemiah. Because of the Levites' activity, interest in the Pentateuch and other books became universal in

Judaism. Their fascination with and reverence for their Scriptures would earn for the Jews the sobriquet "People of the Book."

In outlying regions of Judah and in the lands of the Diaspora (dispersion) where Jews who had not gone to Babylon settled, teaching and reading of the sacred writings eventually served as a substitute for temple worship. There was only one temple—that in Jerusalem—but there sprang up numerous "synagogues" (from the Greek *syn*, meaning "together," and *agein*, meaning "to bring"). The synagogues became meeting houses where the Law and the Prophets were read, pondered, studied and interpreted by *rabbis* ("teachers").

Significantly, it was during this time also that Hebrew began to fade out as the Jews' spoken language. In Palestine the Jews began to speak first Aramaic and later both Aramaic and Greek. In Egypt and other lands of the Diaspora, Jewish children grew up learning the native tongue of their particular homeland. Hebrew now had to be taught by rabbis to Jewish boys, who made a conscious effort to learn it.

Further, an era was beginning when Jewish Scripture was sometimes originally written in Greek or some other language instead of Hebrew. (As we shall see in Chapter Thirteen, the original language in which the Jewish Scriptures were written played a large part in determining the difference between Protestant and Catholic versions of the Old Testament.)

This brief sketch of the history of Restoration Judah perhaps suggests that the Israelites' traditional religious problems had been laid to rest with Ezra's establishment of the Pentateuch as the source book of the Jewish religion. Such is not the case. The Jews did not escape their most enduring dilemma: how to live their faith in a land dominated by pagan values.

The problem of religious syncretism continued to ensnare the Jews, just as it had threatened the first band of desert nomads who followed Joshua into the Promised Land. Many returning Jews quickly married foreigners and adapted their religion to the demands of pagan customs. As a result, a major aspect of the teaching of Ezra the priest and Nehemiah the governor was the condemnation of intermarriage with pagans. Ezra called for the Jews to divorce their foreign wives (Ezr 9—10), while Nehemiah taught only that no *new* mixed marriages were to be contracted (Neh 13).

Because of the Jewish proscription against mixed marriage, Judaism entered into a period of exclusivism. Second-Isaiah's universalist dream of all nations streaming to Jerusalem, accepting Yahweh as their Lord, was transformed by Jews of Ezra's time into concern with religious purity and segregation from pagan ways.

This exclusivist tendency in Judaism was not motivated by racial or religious *prejudice,* as we understand that term today. It was simply a commonsense, practical effort to foster the tender shoot of developing Judaism. As we shall see in Chapter Thirteen, there existed alongside this mentality of segregation the opposite impulse of cosmopolitanism, represented by the Jewish wisdom literature.

LAST OF THE OLD TESTAMENT PROPHETS

Besides the temptation of religious syncretism, another traditional religious problem reasserted itself during the restoration period. Just as their ancestors had done centuries before in the time of Micah and Isaiah, Jews living in restored Judah began to abuse the poor and less fortunate in their midst.

Malachi

Echoing the words of Micah centuries before, the prophet Malachi rebuked the Jews for their injustice and for perverting the spirit of temple worship. Through the prophet, Yahweh addressed the people:

> I mean to visit you for the judgment and I am going to be a ready witness against sorcerer, adulterer, and perjurer, against those who oppress the wage-earner, the widow and the orphan, and who rob the settler of his rights.... (Mal 3:5)

Malachi condemned the people for perverting the temple cult by offering only the scrawniest animals in sacrifice. Their false religious devotion mirrored their social lives, where divorce (of Jewish wives) was practiced for flimsy reasons. "I hate people to parade their sins on their cloaks," Yahweh said through Malachi. "Respect your own life, therefore, and do not break faith like this" (Mal 2:16).

Malachi (writing perhaps in 460 B.C.) represents the last gasp of the classical Israelite prophetic tradition. After him, Obadiah and Joel (c. 400-380 B.C.) were to write in a new genre, developed more fully about the year 325 B.C. by "Second-Zechariah"(Zec 9—14) and brought to full flower in the Book of Daniel. This style of writing is called *apocalyptic* and is the subject of the next chapter.

Second-Zechariah

Let us close this chapter by taking a brief look at Second-Zechariah, whose writings (Zec 9—14), like those of Second-Isaiah, were placed in the book of an earlier prophet whose name he was given.* This anonymous later prophet forms a bridge from the time of the Chronicler to the Greek takeover. He wrote shortly after the Greek conquest of Persia, possibly in the year 325 B.C. Since we have no historical record of the period from the end of the Chronicler's epic (c. 400 B.C.) to the year 325, we know little about the history of Judah during the prophet's time. Yet, we receive clues from the writing of Second-Zechariah itself.

Leadership in Judah evidently fell into chaos. Through Second-Zechariah Yahweh said, "My anger burns against the shepherds" (Zec 10:3)—the leaders of the people. The prophet foresaw Yahweh's coming in power to restore his people who "wander because they have no shepherd" (10:2). Yet, like Second-Isaiah, Second-Zechariah foresaw Yahweh's triumph taking place in a paradoxical fashion:

> Rejoice heart and soul, daughter of Zion!
> Shout with gladness daughter of Jerusalem!
> See now your king comes to you;
> he is victorious, he is triumphant,
> humble and riding a donkey,
> on a colt, the foal of a donkey. (Zec 9:9)

Second-Zechariah's vision of the messianic kingdom was filled with mystery. Yahweh would triumph, but he would do so in the person of someone who was "humble," someone who, like Second-Isaiah's suffering servant, would not "break the crushed reed," or "quench a wavering flame" (Is 42:3), someone who would be "pierced" for the people (Zec 12:10).

Despite the paradoxical fashion in which the messianic age would be ushered in, Second-Zechariah believed fully in its coming. On the day of Yahweh all nations would realize the dominance of the Jews, and the universal supremacy of Yahweh. The enemies of Yahweh's people would be finally and totally destroyed, and eternal peace and prosperity would reign on earth.

We see from the prophecies of Second-Zechariah that the period of Jewish history we have just looked at closed as it began—on a message of triumph, hope and fulfillment. Second-Isaiah (c. 540 B.C.) and Second-Zechariah (c. 325 B.C.) bound the end points of the epic together with cords of optimism. Yahweh would come soon, they taught, to establish his universal reign. No foe would be able to contest him, no enemy stand in his path. Above it all would rise a new

---

*We saw that the prophet named Zechariah lived during the early restoration period (p. 122), some two centuries before Second-Zechariah.

Jerusalem, shining like diamonds in the sun, a beacon of salvation for all people.

On the eve of the Greek takeover of Judah, very few Jews had any intuition of how these messianic prophecies would be fulfilled. Nor did they understand at the time how thoroughly they would first have to experience the negative dimension of these messianic prophecies—the suffering foretold by Second-Isaiah and Second-Zechariah. But as the Jews moved from Persian domination to Greek domination, they soon learned how terribly they would have to suffer for their faith.

CHAPTER THIRTEEN

'ONE LIKE A SON OF MAN'

Daniel, 1 and 2 Maccabees

The history of Judaism during the period of Greek domination reminds one of the old proverb, "The more things change, the more they remain the same." The Jews, it seemed, were forever haunted by the temptation to dilute their faith in Yahweh by mixing pagan elements into their religion. We have seen this pattern in operation throughout Israel's history. In this chapter we will find the Old Testament Jews undergoing the final test of their faith.

We thus come to an account of the definitive challenge to the nation's existence, to the moment when the greatest crisis in Judaism had been reached. Barely two centuries after the events we will now consider, the Jewish state would be destroyed, not to rise again until 1948 when modern Jews would first fly the star of David above the rooftops of Jersualem.

One could easily imagine how Old Testament writers who lived during this period were affected by the national crisis. Just as during the American Revolution we find Thomas Paine urging his compatriots to fight to the last breath, so we find during this period of Jewish history the same kind of patriotic fervor. Paine wrote, "These are the times that try men's souls." His contemporary, Patrick Henry, proclaimed, "Give me liberty or give me death!" Similar sentiments were expressed by the Jewish writers we will consider in this chapter.

Like the American revolutionaries, the Jewish patriots of late Old Testament times knew that their lives were at stake. They knew also that their nation was locked in a struggle whose outcome would bring either life or death for the Jewish faith. To see how this moment of great crisis was reached, let us look for a moment at the history of the ancient Near East.

THE COMING OF THE GREEKS

In the year 333 B.C. the history of the ancient world was pointed in a new direction. A young warlord from Macedonia, Alexander the Great, defeated the Persians at the battle of Issus and consolidated his hold on Asia Minor. He then set out to conquer the known world, following his desire to form all peoples into a single Greek empire. Alexander died 10 years later in Babylon, weeping over the fact that there were no more worlds to conquer. During his brief military career he had brought all of Asia Minor under the domination of Greek power.

Empire-building was nothing new in ancient history. What distinguished Alexander from his bellicose and power-hungry predecessors was the way in which his conquest influenced the people he subdued. All previous conquerors had been Asian. Alexander was a European. All previous conquerors had come from cultures based on the supremacy of mystery over reason and religion over science. Alexander, who had studied at the feet of Aristotle, believed in the triumph of rationalism over religion and human individualism over the angry power of the gods.

This, of course, is a great generalization. Alexander and the Greeks had their gods and their mystery cults, too. But compared to the Asians, the Greeks stood for a bold new type of thinking which can best be summarized by saying that, in Greek thought, human reason was more important than religious faith.

Just as after World War II the modern world entered the "American era," so after the death of Alexander the ancient world entered the "Greek era." Just as many countries liberated by American GI's rushed to adopt various aspects of American culture, so many ancient peoples became enamored of the new Greek culture which Alexander's soldiers left behind them.

Not everyone, of course, was attracted to the new ways. Just as many modern Europeans began to detest the corruption of their ancient customs by the American "hot-dog and drug-store" culture, many ancient peoples likewise began to wonder whether Greek ways were good for them after all. Nowhere was the conflict between new ways and old more noticeable than in Judah.

Like their pagan neighbors, many Jews were entranced by the new Greek ideas. Rationalism, science, philosophy—these were heady topics for a people whose entire life was bound up with religious Scripture and the temple cult. Many young Jews in particular became intoxicated by the new ideas.

A serious cleavage in Jewish religious practice thus developed during the period following Alexander's conquest. One group of Jews insisted on the old ways and looked upon Greek ideas as perverse. Another group went wholeheartedly over to Greek culture, repudiating their Jewish faith and Jewish ancestry altogether. A third group—"the Hellenizers"—tried to compromise, maintaining there need be no conflict between Judaism and Greek culture. This latter group even included some of the Jewish high priests.

When Alexander died, his empire was divided into four parts, with a different Greek family appointed to rule each part. The two ruling families which affect our story were the Ptolemies and the Seleucids, whose respective capitals were Alexandria in Egypt and Antioch in Syria. The Ptolemies controlled Judah (and all of Palestine) until 201 B.C., when the Seleucid King Antiochus III defeated the Ptolemies in battle and assumed control of Palestine. This was to have drastic consequences for the Jews.

The Ptolemies had never insisted that the Jews adopt Greek culture. With the coming to power of the Seleucids, however, this began to change, if only in subtle ways at first. Jews were increasingly forced by the Hellenization programs of the Seleucids to choose between their ancient faith and the new Greek ways. More and more Jews renounced their Judaism—or tried to compromise it—by becoming good citizens of the Seleucid kings.

Jews began to change their names from traditional Hebrew names like *Joshua* to Greek names like *Jason*. Jewish athletes, before competing in the Greek games in which everyone competed naked, had their circumcision covered up by surgery—that is, they renounced the ancient sign of the Abrahamic covenant (Gn 17:9-14) which they carried on their bodies. This was but one example of how Jews betrayed their allegiance to Yahweh.

Just as the American nation at the time of the Civil War could not exist "half slave and half free," neither could the Jewish state long continue "half Jew and half Greek." Matters came to a head with the accession to the Seleucid throne of King Antiochus IV (175-164 B.C.), nicknamed *Epiphanes,* or "God manifest." Antiochus was not content to let some of the Jews choose Greek ways and some remain faithful to the old ways. He began an aggressive policy of Hellenization, *forcing* Jews under penalty of death to renounce fundamental elements of their faith. Offering sacrifice in the temple, circumcision of newborn boys and reading the Pentateuch were among the many traditional Jewish observances declared capital offenses. Antiochus Epiphanes virtually declared war on Judaism. Left unchallenged, he no doubt would have wiped the Yahweh faith from the face of the earth.

But challengers there were—on two fronts: one military and the other theological. The conservative Maccabee family rallied Jews to oppose Antiochus with force of arms. The writer of the Book of Daniel (Dn) wrote to teach his compatriots the theological significance of Antiochus' attack on the Jewish faith and to assure them that even Antiochus' persecution was a part of Yahweh's universal plan. The scriptural sources we shall consider in this chapter are the Book of Daniel (Dn), First Book of Maccabees (1 Mc) and the Second Book of Maccabees (2 Mc).

A DIGRESSION: WHAT BOOKS BELONG IN THE OT?

With our consideration of 1 and 2 Maccabees and Daniel, we notice for the first time a divergence between Protestant and Catholic versions of the Old Testament. The latter contains both 1 and 2 Maccabees; the former contains neither. In addition, Catholic Old Testaments contain sections of Daniel that are not included in Protestant Old Testaments—specifically, Dn 3:24-90 and Dn 13 and 14. Before we can look more fully at these books, we must first consider how it is that the Protestant and Catholic traditions came to differ on which Jewish writings should be included in the Old Testament.

The origins of this divergence lie in the phenomenon known as the *Diaspora*. As we have seen (see p. 124), this term refers to the "dispersion" of Jews into foreign lands at the time of the Exile.

One of the principal centers of the Jewish Diaspora was Alexandria, Egypt. By the time of the Greek takeover in Judah, several generations of Jews in Alexandria had already grown up speaking Greek rather than Hebrew as their native tongue. Their reliance on Greek had become so dominant that they eventually translated the Pentateuch and other Hebrew Scriptures into Greek so that the sacred writings could be more easily understood by Greek-speaking Jews in Egypt and elsewhere in the Diaspora. The Jews living in the Diaspora frequently included in the newly translated version of their Scriptures more recent religious literature *originally written* in Greek by Alexandrian Jewish writers.

Writing Jewish Scripture in Greek was not confined to Alexandria, however. Even in Judah, Jewish writers would often write in Greek instead of Hebrew. We see a clear example of the use of different languages by late Old Testament writers when we examine Daniel and 1 and 2 Maccabees. Daniel was written in three different languages: Dn 1:1—2:4a and 8—12 in Hebrew; Dn 2:4b—7:28 in Aramaic; and the "Catholic sections" we noted earlier in Greek. The First Book of Maccabees was written originally in Hebrew. The ancient Hebrew text has vanished and today we have only a Greek copy of the original. The Second Book of Maccabees, on the other hand, was written *originally* in Greek.

These examples of the different languages used by Jewish writers in late Old Testament times should suggest to us the problem which the Jews faced when they decided, around 90 A.D., to put together their final, approved collection of authentic Jewish Scriptures.

The rabbis responsible for compiling the "official Jewish Bible" chose only those books which had circulated prominently in the Hebrew language. That was not their only criterion, since some books originally written in Hebrew were omitted from the Jewish "canon" of Scripture. (The word *canon* connotes "norm" or "standard.") For our purposes, however, the fact of most significance is that the rabbis omitted from their canon some of the more recently composed literature which had circulated mostly in Greek.

Several of these Greek books found their way into early Christian Old Testaments for reasons which we need not go into here. The most famous instance of this took place in the late fourth-century A.D., when St. Jerome produced the famous Latin Vulgate edition of the Bible. In his translation, Jerome included many of the Greek books which had been omitted by the rabbis from the Jewish canon 300 years earlier.

The Latin Vulgate became the principal Bible of the Christian Church until the Protestant Reformation of the 16th century, when Protestants began to adopt versions of the Old Testament based strictly on the original Jewish canon. Catholics, on the other hand, continued to use the Vulgate, including the Greek Scriptures which Jerome had included in his translation. (Protestant and Catholic *New* Testaments are identical in the books which they contain.)

Without dwelling any longer on this matter, let us simply list the books found in Catholic versions of the Old Testament and omitted from Protestant versions: Tobit, Judith, Wisdom, Ecclesiasticus (Sirach), Baruch, 1 and 2 Maccabees and parts of Daniel and Esther. This necessary digression aside, let us return now to our consideration of Daniel and 1 and 2 Maccabees.

DANIEL

The Book of Daniel may be divided into two different sections according to the type of writing found in each section. The first section, Dn 1—6 and 13—14, we can label "stories," and the second section, Dn 7—12, we can call "visions." The stories were written sometime during the *early* part of the Greek period (c. 300 B.C.); the visions were written later (c. 164 B.C.), when Antiochus Epiphanes had come to the Seleucid throne. The fact that these two sections were composed in different time periods has a lot to do with the styles of writing and the underlying message we find in each of them.

Both the stories and the visions concern a man named Daniel ("my judge is God" in Hebrew). Daniel was an Israelite of heroic virtue who supposedly lived during the time of the Babylonian Exile. We don't know whether he really existed. But whether Daniel was legendary or historical, the anonymous authors of the two sections of Daniel—who lived a century and a half apart—freely appropriated his personality in their writing for two reasons.

First of all, as was commonly done in ancient times, the authors wanted to associate their teaching with a "famous name." We saw in Chapter One how P put much of his teaching into the mouth of Moses. The authors of Daniel did the same thing. The image of the Israelite folk hero Daniel was strong and positive in Jewish minds; attributing this book to Daniel would increase the chances that the Jews would heed the authors' message.

The second reason why the authors of Daniel used a pseudonym was a very practical one: They wanted their identity to remain a secret. Their ideas would be threatening to the Greek overlords, particularly to the cruel Antiochus, who reigned when the author of the second section of Daniel lived and wrote. Antiochus needed little pretext to put Jews to death. A book which condemned him would furnish all the excuse he needed to execute the author.

In the first section of the book (Dn 1—6), the author's purpose is to help his contemporaries, living under *Greek* domination, by drawing on the experience of Daniel and his three friends, living under *Babylonian* domination. In other words, readers were to identify their situation with that of Daniel and his comrades and profit from the experience of their predecessors. The second section (Dn 7—12) is likewise set in Babylon.

Babylon was used as the setting of Daniel for two reasons: First of all, the Babylonian Exile was the prototype of all pagan domination. Any lessons learned there could be universally applied to other situations where Jews lived in lands controlled by pagans. Secondly, by using Babylon as their model of oppression, the authors of the two sections of Daniel could avoid the peril of making direct reference to wicked Greek rulers. For that reason, the authors structured their account as prophecies from ancient Babylon rather than commentaries on contemporary events in Judah.

The many historical errors to be found in Daniel result from this pretense. For example, in Dn 5, King Belshazzar is erroneously said to be the son of Nebuchadnezzar, when in fact the historical Belshazzar was the son of Nabonidus. Or, as stated in the very first line of Daniel, Jehoiakim was *not* king of Judah when "Nebuchadnezzar king of Babylon marched on Jerusalem and besieged it" (Dn 1:1).

Both authors of Daniel were using the Babylonian era simply as a backdrop to their writing. Their history was imprecise, but that is largely irrelevant to their purpose. The chief purpose of their writing was to bolster the faith of Jews living under Greek domination.

The overall message of Daniel is that the power of Yahweh is supreme even when Jews are subjected to Gentile domination. But the *way* this message is presented differs between the stories and the visions.

The Stories

In the *stories*, the Jews who are challenged by Gentile domination do not cut themselves off from the Gentile culture. As long as the Gentiles allow the Jews to keep their religious traditions intact, the Jews feel perfectly free to live and prosper in Gentile society.

In the stories Daniel, like Joseph in Pharaoh's court (see Gn 41:37-49), thrives in the non-Jewish environment and becomes an official of Nebuchadnezzar's court. He does endure many trials—but all of these trials are concluded victoriously by Yahweh.

The message of Dn 1—6 is that Jews need not oppose Gentile rule as long as they are free to practice their religion. Accommodation to Gentile culture is thus permissible if it does not require the dilution of Judaism with pagan religion.

In the stories, Jewish fidelity even inspires Gentile rulers themselves to acknowledge Yahweh's supremacy. In Dn 6:26-27, for example, King Darius is said to have proclaimed:

> "I decree: in every kingdom of my empire let all tremble with fear before the God of Daniel:
> He is the living God, he endures forever,
> his sovereignty will never be destroyed...." (Dn 6:27)

The Visions

In Dn 7—12 this attitude of "peaceful coexistence" is changed. The author of these "vision" chapters is writing during the time of Antiochus when forced Hellenization had become the law of the land. At this time no compromise between Judaism and paganism was possible for loyal Jews. The very life of Judaism hung in the balance. Loyal Jews needed a theology which would teach them how to exist in a society where they were declared to be enemies of the state.

The writer of chapters 7—12 rose to the occasion. He taught that all of history was encompassed within Yahweh's universal plan. Even the suffering brought about by Antiochus' persecution was part of that plan. Unlike the Deuteronomic theologian, who would have said that the Jews' suffering under Antiochus was a result of Jewish sinfulness, the author of Dn 7—12 makes no such connection. Sinners and righteous alike are seen as part of the same divine plan. Prayer, repentance, fasting are regarded as unnecessary, because God's plan will manifest itself independently of what human beings do.

All of this is so because the struggle is not really between human forces, but between the spiritual powers of good and evil. In the end Yahweh will triumph, conquering all the powers of evil. It is he, and he alone, who will deliver Jews from their oppressors. Thus, according to the author of Dn 7—12, the Jews must seek to learn Yahweh's purpose—and suffer patiently while he accomplishes that purpose.

The writer of Dn 7—12 links his teaching with the messianic prophecies of Second-Isaiah and Second-Zechariah, who likewise predicted Yahweh's final defeat of Judaism's enemies and the ultimate victory of the Jews. In making this link, however, the author employs a different style of writing than we have encountered before: The writer of Dn 7—12 is not a prophet, but an *apocalypticist*.

Apocalyptic literature was a genre that developed during the late Old Testament period. It came to full flower in the Book of Daniel, and in the New Testament Book of Revelation. This type of writing was concerned principally with the cosmic struggle between good and evil.

In reality, apocalyptic writers said, the earthly struggles we see going on all around us are symbolic of the transcendent, universal conflict between the spiritual power of evil and the spiritual power of good. All creation is caught up in this universal warfare between good and evil. Yet Yahweh is in firm control, and on some final day, at the end of all time, he will conquer wickedness once and for all and inaugurate his universal rule in its full glory.

Until that final showdown human beings must choose sides,

opting either for good or for evil. In the interim the righteous will frequently suffer while the wicked will temporarily prosper. In the end, however, the triumph will be Yahweh's, and he will share his universal reign of peace with his elect—those who have remained faithful to him.

Because apocalyptic writers saw the earthly struggle between good and evil as symbolic of a deeper conflict, they relied heavily on symbols in their writing. Attempts to interpret these symbols to make them applicable to persons and events of the 20th century completely miss the point that these symbols apply to events of second-century B.C. Judaism.

The most famous set of symbols is found in Dn 7:1-9, the four beasts. The author meant by these symbols four specific pagan kingdoms: Babylonia, Medea, Persia and the Seleucids. The last "beast"—the Seleucid kingdom of Antiochus—was worse than all the rest in its perversity and wickedness. Out of its head arose 10 horns, symbolizing the 10 kings who ruled before Antiochus. Antiochus is the "little horn" (7:8) which supplanted the 10 horns or kings who went before him.

Out of this collection of beastly symbols suddenly arises a new vision, made up of hopeful, consoling symbols. "One of great age" (7:9), Yahweh himself, comes to judge the nations. The power of Antiochus and his wicked cohorts is broken and is replaced by the power of a new figure, "one like a son of man" (7:13):

> "On him was conferred sovereignty,
>   glory and kingship.
> and men of all peoples, nations and languages became his servants.
> His sovereignty is an eternal sovereignty
> which shall never pass away,
> nor will his empire ever be destroyed." (Dn 7:14)

Who is this "one like a son of man"? Placed as it is in opposition to the symbols of the four beasts, the symbol of the son of man stands for a nation of righteousness which supplants the reign of the wicked nations. The son of man symbolizes victorious Israel, heir to the ancient messianic throne promised long ago in David's time. He assumes the throne held up in faith to the Jews by the great prophets for generations. The symbol further stands for Israel's angelic protector, Michael, who is appointed by Yahweh to fight for Israel against the spiritual foes who serve the Gentile nations. In a sense, the symbol of the son of man as people and as the angel Michael means the same thing, since it was believed that a nation's protective angel summarized in his person the entire body of the people.

Through the use of symbolism, therefore, the author in Dn 7—12 encourages the faith of his fellow persecuted Jews. The effect of the symbols he used would have been powerful. Jews reading these passages could not have remained depressed about their condition for long. Yahweh would eventually triumph, and all history would end on that triumphant note, leaving the Jews as masters of the nations.

1 AND 2 MACCABEES

The rather passive theology of Daniel did not require the Jews to take any action to advance their own cause. This stands in marked contrast to the world view advanced by 1 and 2 Maccabees. The authors of these two books must have looked upon the Book of Daniel as "pie-in-the-sky" theology. Instead of counseling the Jews to wait patiently for Yahweh to take control of things, these two writers urged the Jews to take up arms and fight their oppressors. And instead of looking forward to the age of an ethereal "son of man," they believed that the best hope for the Jews lay in allying themselves with the Maccabee family, whose history these books recount, and in supporting the Maccabees' aggressive tactics.

The books of 1 and 2 Maccabees, like several other books in the Old Testament—Leviticus and Chronicles, for example—are very easy to put down. They are not great literature. Catholics reading these books should be able to sympathize with the Protestant reformers who excised these books from the Old Testament because they often read more like political propaganda than "holy writ." Nevertheless, 1 and 2 Maccabees do help us to round out our understanding of late Old Testament writing.

Different authors wrote 1 and 2 Maccabees. The second book is not a continuation of the first, but a separate work in itself. Both, however, are concerned with the same general theme: the rise to power of the Maccabee family and its leadership in the Jewish struggle against Seleucid persecution.

As we have seen, 1 Maccabees was written originally in Hebrew, 2 Maccabees in Greek. The First Book of Maccabees begins with the first days of King Antiochus Epiphanes (175 B.C.) and ends with the accession to the Jewish high priesthood of John Hyrcanus (134 B.C.). The historical period covered in 2 Maccabees is the same, but the story cuts off a little earlier, in the year 161 B.C. There is thus some overlap in the two books, particularly in 1 Mc 3—7 and 2 Mc 8—15, which recount essentially the same details. What follows is the broad outline of Maccabean family history presented in the two books.

When Antiochus Epiphanes began his terrible persecution of the Jews in 167 B.C., many loyal Jews refused to capitulate to his demands to compromise their Jewish faith. Chief among these were the Maccabee family of Modein. Mattathias, the patriarch of this family, triggered a Jewish revolt when he refused to offer sacrifice to a Greek god and killed the king's official in the process (1 Mc 2:23-26). Mattathias was supported by his five sons. Upon Mattathias' death in 166 B.C., the leadership of the revolt passed to his son Judas.

Both 1 and 2 Maccabees make it clear that the Seleucid persecution was facilitated by the treason and infidelity of Jewish Hellenizers—Jews sympathetic to Greek ways. There were even high priests among this latter group, the most famous of whom was Menelaus (notice his Greek name), who had attained his office by bribing Antiochus. The authors are particularly harsh in their condemnation of these Jewish quislings. In 2 Maccabees Menelaus is called "the chief enemy of his fellow citizens" (2 Mc 4:50). Thus, the Maccabean wars were not just military ventures against Gentiles. They also represented an attempt by conservative Jews to purge Judaism of those elements which stood for compromise with Greek culture.

Judas Maccabaeus won victory after victory during his tenure as Jewish commander-in-chief. When Antiochus died in 164 B.C., claimants to the Seleucid throne, regularly murdering each other off, destroyed the internal cohesion of Seleucid power. As a result, the Maccabees were able to play one rival Seleucid faction off against another.

Jonathan Maccabaeus succeeded to Maccabee family leadership in 160 B.C. upon the death of his brother Judas. During Jonathan's tenure of leadership (160-142 B.C.), the Maccabees were able to hold their own with the Seleucids. Antiochus' successor, King Alexander Balas, had to admit the growth in Maccabean power and even appointed Jonathan Jewish high priest. Thus began a new era in the Maccabean family history.

When Jonathan was succeeded by his brother Simon, the Jews at last entered an era of stability and independence from foreign domination. Under Simon, the various Jewish factions accepted the Maccabean claim to the high priesthood, and the Maccabean hold on this office became hereditary. Simon served as high priest from 143-134 B.C. and was followed in office by his son John Hyrcanus. At that point, 1 Maccabees terminates its history.

This brief outline ignores many details of the story which are sacred in Jewish memories. One of the high points in all of Jewish history is found in 1 Mc 4:36-60, where we read of Judas' rededication of the temple. The scene described is the first Hanukkah celebration, a feast which would become as important to the Jews as Passover. The climax of 2 Maccabees is the martyrdom of seven Jewish brothers (2 Mc 7), an example of courage and religious fidelity which exceeds anything like it in the Old Testament.

The theological message of 1 and 2 Maccabees appears on virtually every page of these books: that Jews must resist religious persecution by force and, if necessary, lay down their lives to keep Judaism undefiled by paganism. The two books differ, however, on the issue of the final outcome of Jewish resistance.

PERSONAL RESURRECTION: A BRIDGE TO THE NEW TESTAMENT

The author of 1 Maccabees sees Jewish resistance leading to the establishment of an independent Jewish political state led by the Maccabean family. The author of 2 Maccabees, while not opposed to the establishment of such a state, holds out an even greater reward to loyal Jewish resisters. That reward is a personal resurrection from the dead. This is a belief which 2 Maccabees shares with the Book of Daniel. The optimistic conclusion of Dn 12 is that the good will rise from the dead and will somehow share the glorious life of God's holy angels. This first unequivocal assertion of belief in personal immortality in the Old Testament is echoed in 2 Mc 7, the story of the seven brothers.

The respective authors of 2 Maccabees and Daniel thus held up to their persecuted brothers and sisters a greater hope than mere political supremacy. If you will remain steadfast to the end, these authors urged their fellow Jews, you will win an eternal reward greater than anything that mere political or military power can achieve.

With this idea, Old Testament theology was on the verge of passing into New Testament theology. All it lacked was one final piece, the teaching of Israel's greatest rabbi, who proclaimed:

"I am the resurrection.
If anyone believes in me, even though he dies he will live,
and whoever lives and believes in me
will never die." (Jn 11:25-26)

CHAPTER FOURTEEN

'WISDOM INSTRUCTS HER CHILDREN'

**Song of Songs, Proverbs, Job,
Ecclesiastes, Ecclesiasticus, Wisdom**

O ur account of Israel's life story has thus far been rather "events-oriented." This approach was necessitated by organizing our material according to the chronology of the Old Testament's composition. Yet the life of a people is more than events.

Really to get to know a people, we must step back from the chronological flow of events and enter into their lives at individual moments of their existence. We must remove ourselves from *chronos* and enter into *kairos* with the people we wish to know. We must stop our activity and listen to their deep thoughts and feelings.

The best way to do this with people far removed from us in time is to study the literature in which they reveal such feelings and thoughts. In the Old Testament we are blessed with three special categories of writing which help us to get in touch with the people of Israel in this way. In this and our two concluding chapters we will examine these categories: the wisdom literature, the short stories and the psalms.

The wisdom books of the Old Testament include Proverbs, Job, Ecclesiastes and—in Catholic Old Testaments only—Ecclesiasticus (also called Sirach in some translations of the Bible) and Wisdom. The Song of Songs and Psalms are also traditionally listed among the wisdom books, but in this discussion, we will reserve Psalms for separate consideration in Chapter Sixteen. Let us begin our overview of the wisdom literature by looking at the *origins* of the Old Testament wisdom tradition.

FOCUS ON THE INDIVIDUAL

If we were to try to draw one single conclusion about Israelite history from the Exodus to the Maccabean revolt, it would be this: Israelite life was *communal* in nature.

The great events of Israel's history were events in which Yahweh related to the *entire people*. He formed a *people* in the desert and called a *people* to be his very own at Mt. Sinai. Even when the nation accepted the leadership of kings, it was always clear that a given king represented in his person the entire body of the people; no single individual, not even a king, could come between Yahweh and the community of all Israelites.

The great prophets repeatedly stressed the corporate nature of Israel's election and salvation. Hosea, for example, compared the Yahweh-Israel relationship to a marriage bond: Yahweh took the entire people to be his very own, in the same way as a husband takes to himself a wife. Yahweh chose and related to the Israelites as a collective entity—and not as a loose aggregation of single individuals, some of whom Yahweh saved and some of whom he did not.

This concept of Israel *as unit* affected every aspect of its national existence. In particular, it affected religious literature. Every Old Testament book we have considered so far was concerned with telling some segment of Israel's story as a community. For that reason, communal interests and communal values are predominant in those books.

Wisdom literature differs from other Old Testament literature in this respect. The wisdom tradition concerns itself less with Israel as community and more with Israelites as individual human beings. The focus in wisdom writing is on the inner workings of the individual human personality, rather than on the external realities of Israel's life as a nation. To see how and why wisdom literature took this approach, we must return for a moment to the time of Solomon.

King Solomon's Court

During King Solomon's era, Israel for the first time became a respected international power—by no means a *great* power in comparison to the superpowers of the day, but a nation to be reckoned with nevertheless. One of the outgrowths of Israel's entrance into international politics was the establishment of economic and cultural ties with the surrounding nations. Israel for the first time rubbed shoulders with such traditional mighty empires as Egypt.

It was natural for the Israelites—who were newcomers to

monarchical politics—to imitate the customs and practices of the kingdoms with which they related. "After all," they thought, "there must be a certain etiquette and style to this kingship business, and we don't want to look like rubes in the big city when it comes to running our new kingdom."

This type of thinking led Israelite officials visiting foreign lands earnestly to study those writings which would tell them how a monarchical state was to conduct its affairs. Particularly in Egypt Israelite emissaries found a rich tradition of literature pertaining to life at court. They brought such writings back with them to Solomon's court, where they were eagerly studied for content and style.

One such Egyptian work was the *Instruction of Amenemopet,* originally written in the form of a teaching given by a learned elder to a young nobleman trying to learn proper conduct for life at the king's court. The emphasis in the elder's instruction was on how the young man could mold his behavior so as to become wise.

When Israelite writers began to compose their own wisdom literature—keeping it always within the confines of the Yahweh faith—they retained in their writing the Egyptian style and the Egyptian emphasis on individual moral conduct. For example, the Book of Proverbs (Prv) is cast in the form of instructions from father to son, and the instructions given deal with the same practical questions addressed by the Egyptian work cited above.

Israel's Sages

This type of writing became the special concern of Israel's own sages who, as a result of their interest in the study of human psychology and the natural world, gradually became a separate class of teachers and advisors. By the time of Jeremiah, Israel's sages, or wise men, had evidently achieved the same status in Israelite society as priests and prophets (Jer 18:18).

These sages provided teachings on aspects of Israelite life not covered by the teaching of either the Law or the Prophets—both of which were concerned principally with Israel's *communal* relationship to Yahweh. The sages were interested in giving *individuals* practical advice for everyday living. They did not see themselves as opposed to, or outside of, the traditions of the community, but they focused on the individual's relationship with Yahweh rather than the community's. As a result, they dealt with questions previously ignored in Old Testament writing.

One of these questions concerned the notion of worldly success, which led by logical extension to a concern with the meaning and purpose of existence and to the question of immortality. Heretofore Old Testament writers had understood such concepts only as they applied to the people as a collective entity. The people were seen as blessed for their righteousness or cursed for their sins. Likewise, it was the people who were saved by Yahweh and the people as a whole who would achieve a state of continued existence. Individual existence terminated at death, it was thought, while the nation lived on forever—in the sense that parents lived on perpetually in their children.

The wisdom writers looked into these matters more deeply and began to ask questions and reach conclusions that were to point the Jewish faith in a new direction.

WISDOM BOOKS: AN OVERVIEW

Reading wisdom literature is similar in one respect to reading prophetic literature: There is no logical arrangement of the material. If you were to approach Proverbs, for example, expecting to follow a central theme developed in order from beginning to end, you would be most disappointed. Proverbs is a collection of collections, written over centuries and stitched together in its final form perhaps as late as the third century B.C.

As a result, reading Proverbs—and Wisdom and Ecclesiasticus too, for that matter—is not like reading a structured essay. These three works are more similar to reference books than to essays. Just as we would not sit down to read *Webster's Third International Dictionary* or Bartlett's *Familiar Quotations* straight through, neither should we approach Proverbs, Wisdom or Ecclesiasticus in this fashion. The teaching of these books is meant to be absorbed in small doses over long periods of time, to be savored, internalized and put into action in specific instances in one's life. A quick reading of Proverbs, Wisdom and Ecclesiasticus will certainly not make one wise.

The other wisdom books—Job, Ecclesiastes and Song of Songs—are more thematic than the three referred to above. Each deals more or less with one central idea. Song of Songs, although placed with the wisdom books in the Old Testament, in actuality concerns itself with a different theme than the other five—a theme which admits of various interpretations. Some scholars believe that it is purely and simply what it professes to be: an erotic love poem celebrating the sanctity and joy of marital union. Some see it as a remembrance of the marriage of Solomon to one of his foreign wives. Others see in it a dialogue between wisdom and the soul. Christian mystics (Bernard and John of the Cross) found in it resonances of their own contemplative experience in which, they believed, God sought union with their souls.

Probably the most common interpretation of Song of Songs, and the one followed by the early Church Fathers, is allegorical. In this interpretation the lover is Yahweh and the beloved is Yahweh's people Israel; the poem is thus principally a celebration of Yahweh's love for his people. The early Christian Church substituted Christ for Yahweh and the Church for Israel in this formulation. The strength of this interpretation lies in the long tradition which conceives Yahweh's relationship with his people as primarily a love relationship. This tradition is perhaps best exemplified in Hos 1—3. Third-Isaiah repeats this theme (62:5), as do Jeremiah (3:1-10), and Ezekiel (16, 23).

Whatever the "correct interpretation" of Song of Songs, one thing is clear: Both sexual love and the human body are presented in the poem as beautiful and good. Perhaps this is why Song of Songs is traditionally associated with the wisdom books.

Like much of the wisdom literature, Song of Songs is concerned with the experience of human joy and happiness. Jews of Old Testament times did not divide human nature, as we do today, into body and spirit. A person was seen as an integrated whole. The body was never seen as being in opposition to spirit, or of less worth than spirit, as was the case in some dualistic Oriental religions. The body, sex, indeed all of material creation, were seen by the Jews as good.

This belief in the goodness of creation explains why much of the wisdom literature is concerned with achieving earthly success. Proverbs, in particular, presents wealth almost as if it were a religious virtue:

> The rich man's wealth is his stronghold,
> poverty is the poor man's undoing. (Prv 10:15)

> The poor man is detestable even to his neighbor,
> but the rich man has friends and to spare. (Prv 14:20)

Because of their desire to offer practical advice on how to achieve the "good life"—which was always understood within the context of strict Judaism—the wisdom writers probed deeply into the end result of earthly success. Like many people today, the wisdom writers wanted to know, "What's it all about?" This inquiry into the purpose and end of human existence brought the wisdom writers to varying conclusions.

In Proverbs, for example, we find a conservative presentation of traditional Deuteronomic thought: Rewards and blessings come to the good; misfortune and unhappiness are the lot of the wicked.

The house of the wicked shall be destroyed,
the tent of honest men will stand firm. (Prv 14:11)

In the house of the virtuous there is no lack of treasure,
the earnings of the wicked are fraught with anxiety. (Prv 15:6)

The fear of Yahweh leads to life,
a man has food and shelter, and no evil to fear. (Prv 19:23)

A NEW VIEW OF GOOD AND EVIL

This linking of virtue with wealth, and wickedness with
poverty, was to receive a strong challenge from another wisdom
writer—one who wrote what many consider to be the finest piece of
literature in all the Old Testament.

The Challenge of Job

The author of the Book of Job (Jb) was troubled by the ancient
Deuteronomic formulation. Writing in postexilic times, probably in the
fifth century B.C., he wanted to challenge the facile association of
wealth with virtue and poverty with wickedness. As result, he presents
the story of Job, "a sound and honest man who feared God and shunned
evil" (Jb 1:1). When Job's many material blessings are taken away
from him, the scene is set for a contest between the traditional
understanding of divine retribution—as represented in the words of
Eliphaz, Bildad and Zophar—and Job's groping search for a deeper
understanding of God's ways.

Job's three friends confidently assert that Job's misfortune is a
result of his sinfulness. "It is a man who breeds trouble for himself"
(Jb 5:7), Eliphaz tells Job. "Do not refuse this lesson from Shaddai
[God]" (Jb 5:17). Bildad chimes in,

"God neither spurns a stainless man,
nor lends his aid to the evil...." (Jb 8:20)

Zophar, Job's third friend, succinctly summarizes the traditional
position when he says, "It is for sin [that God] calls you to account"
(Jb 11:6).

The discourses of Eliphaz, Bildad and Zophar thus present the
conservative theological position, familiar to anyone who has read the
Deuteronomic writings in the Old Testament.

The fatal flaw in this way of thinking was that God's ways were
reduced to a mechanical formulation. In this viewpoint there is no more
mystery to God than there is in the operation of a vending machine.

146

God operates according to strict mechanical principle, just as one puts a coin in a machine and receives a candy bar. In this traditional view of good and evil, God reacts exactly according to a script—on time, and in the exact place specified. God is stripped of all mystery; he is merely a projection of a person's own thoughts.

The Book of Job was a reaction against this mechanistic theology. Job bitterly protests his innocence in the face of his friends' condemnation and issues a strong challenge to their glib formulations. Eventually, however, he gives up all hope of convincing his friends and cries out to God himself, challenging *him* to give an answer to the question of why the good suffer:

> You, who inquire into my faults
> and investigate my sins,
> You know very well that I am innocent....
> You attack, and attack me again,
> with stroke on stroke of your fury....
> "Why did you bring me out of the womb?..." (Jb 10:6-7a, 17-18a)

After a long series of discourses in which Job constantly reasserts his righteousness before God, the Almighty finally answers. At first God's answer seems like a non-answer. Instead of telling Job, "Here is why you and other good people suffer and why those three friends of yours are wrong"—which is what Job wanted to hear—God launches into an account of his own wisdom, power and majesty. God asks Job,

> Have you ever in your life given orders to the morning
> or sent the dawn to its post?...
> Have you ever visited the place where the snow is kept,
> or seen where the hail is stored up?...
> Can you fasten the harness of the Pleiades,
> or untie Orion's bands? (Jb 38:12, 22, 31)

We might summarize this encounter between Job and God by imagining Job saying, "But, God, I don't understand," to which God replies, "I *know* you don't." In other words, the conclusion of Job is a challenge—a challenge to the traditional Deuteronomic formulation as well as to all those who think that they have God figured out.

At the conclusion of Job, the reader realizes that God is and will remain a mystery, despite human attempts to fit God into a neatly packaged framework. Job, like all of us, must submit to the mystery of God in faith. The author of Job thus asserts the supremacy of the

Almighty against human finiteness and smallness.

The author's purpose in Job was not to write a clever theodicy. Rather, he urged surrender in faith to God's omnipotence, believing that humanity should not assert its righteousness or demand from God recompense for virtue. Thus *both* Job and his friends were in error—the latter for imagining that their health and well-being were signs of their virtue, and Job for thinking that by his virtue he could call God to account.

Job is changed by the encounter with God. He has gone through the desert with God and come out a new man:

> I have been holding forth on matters I cannot understand,
>> on marvels beyond me and my knowledge....
> I knew you then only by hearsay;
>> but now, having seen you with my own eyes,
> I retract all I have said
>> and in dust and ashes I repent. (Jb 42:3, 5-6)

'Vanity, Vanity...'

Like the author of Job, the author of Ecclesiastes (Eccl) also challenged D's theology. Contrary to the teaching of the traditional viewpoint he wrote, "I observe that under the sun crime is where law should be, the criminal where the good should be" (Eccl 3:16). His conclusion was that "all is vanity" (3:19). Since human life ends at the grave, "there is no happiness for man but to be happy in his work" (3:22). In this respect Ecclesiastes is similar to Job, which taught that a person "dies, and lifeless he remains" (Jb 14:10).

Job and Ecclesiastes may be regarded as pessimistic responses to the question of human existence. Whereas Proverbs optimistically saw religious faith and personal prosperity going hand in hand, Job and Ecclesiastes stressed the illusory nature of material possessions. Even though Proverbs offered no hope in an afterlife, it at least exalted the material benefits which come from living a good life. Job and Ecclesiastes, on the other hand, held up the transitory nature of material wealth *as well as* the hopelessness of looking for virtue's reward beyond the grave. We see the final Old Testament solution to the questions concerning divine retribution and personal immortality by turning to the Book of Ecclesiasticus (Sir) and the Book of Wisdom (Wis).

A FINAL SOLUTION

Protestant Old Testaments exclude these two books. Thus their collection of wisdom literature ends on the rather gloomy note of Ecclesiastes, which was written sometime during the early part of the Greek domination of Palestine. By including Ecclesiasticus and Wisdom, Catholic Old Testaments follow the Jewish wisdom movement to a later point in time.

Ecclesiasticus was written a decade or two before the Maccabean revolt, perhaps around the year 180 B.C. Wisdom was composed at a later date, well after the Maccabean family had achieved supremacy in Judah. Possibly written as late as the year 50 B.C., it is the latest piece of Old Testament writing we have.

Both Ecclesiasticus and Wisdom are concerned with the problem of Hellenization, and both want to teach their readers that the wisdom given by Yahweh is superior to the human philosophy of the Greeks. Both books were written by Jews who lived in the Jewish community in Alexandria. Wisdom was written in Greek. Ecclesiasticus, written originally in Hebrew by Jesus ben Sira, was translated by his grandson into Greek.

Because of the name of the original author, the *New American Bible* calls this book Sirach rather than Ecclesiasticus, which is the name the *Jerusalem Bible* uses. (We use the abbreviation *Sir* here.) The name *Ecclesiasticus* stems from the Greek word for *Church,* which suggests the book's early usage as "the Church's book."

Ecclesiasticus reminds us somewhat of Proverbs, since the bulk of it contains pithy teachings on practical wisdom—which, like those in Proverbs, are for the most part not organized according to any particular plan. Wisdom, on the other hand, reads a bit more like an integrated discourse.

The chief difference between Ecclesiasticus and Wisdom and the earlier wisdom literature, however, is that these books express much of their teaching in the language of a philosophically-oriented culture rather than a religiously-oriented one. The genius of these two authors is that they are able to write within a philosphical milieu and still emphasize the superiority of traditional Jewish teaching over Greek philosophy. The author of Ecclesiasticus, for example, underscores the supremacy of traditional Judaism by equating wisdom with the Law. After a long discourse on the nature of wisdom, the author concludes:

> All this is no other than the book of the covenant of the Most High God, the law that Moses enjoined on us. (Sir 24:23*)

---

*Slightly different numbering for verses in Sirach is used in other translations. For example in the New American Bible, Sir 24:23 is Sir 24:22.

Wisdom is thus not to be found in philosophy; rather, "Wisdom is entirely constituted by the fulfilling of the Law" (Sir 19:20b).

We find another example in Ecclesiasticus of traditional Jewish thinking. Ecclesiasticus supports the ancient view that life ends with the grave, referring to the dead as "those who do not exist" (Sir 17:28). Because of the traditional view on human mortality in Ecclesiasticus we find there traces of the old teaching on divine retribution:

> [T]he sinner shall not escape with his ill-gotten gains,
>> nor the devout man's patience go for nothing. (Sir 16:13-14)

Yet the author's handling of this subject is much more nuanced than the treatment of this same subject in Proverbs. The author of Ecclesiasticus had no doubt studied the teachings of Job and Ecclesiastes. He was leery of presenting the idea of retribution as if there were an absolute correspondence between a virtuous life and material prosperity:

> Many monarchs have been made to sit on the ground,
>> and the man nobody thought of has worn the crown.
> Many influential men have been utterly disgraced,
>> and prominent men have fallen into the power of others. (Sir 11:5-6)

It remained to the author of the Book of Wisdom to bring Jewish wisdom literature more into line with the view of divine retribution and personal immortality already advanced by the author of Dn 7—12.

As we saw in the last chapter, Dn 7—12 (written between the times of Ecclesiasticus and Wisdom) was the first Old Testament writing to state unequivocally that the life of the good person did not end at death. The author of Wisdom continues this theme. Using the concept of the soul—which he borrowed from Greek philosophy—he gives the final Old Testament solution to the question of human immortality and divine retribution. The author of Wisdom combines the realism of Job and Ecclesiastes with the optimism of Proverbs and Ecclesiasticus. He points the teaching of these books toward a vision of everlasting blessing for the virtuous:

> But the souls of the virtuous are in the hands of God,
> no torment shall ever touch them.
> In the eyes of the unwise, they did appear to die,
> their going looked like a disaster,
> their leaving us, like annihilation;
> but they are in peace.
> If they experienced punishment as men see it,
> their hope was rich with immortality;

slight was their affliction, great will their blessings be.
God has put them to the test
and proved them worthy to be with him;
he has tested them like gold in a furnace,
and accepted them as a holocaust.
When the time comes for his visitation they will shine out;
as sparks through the stubble, so will they.
They shall judge nations, rule over peoples,
and the Lord will be their king for ever.
They who trust in him will understand the truth,
those who are faithful will live with him in love;
for grace and mercy await those he has chosen. (Wis 3:1-9)

The challenge to the ancient Deuteronomic formulation issued so eloquently by Job and repeated by Ecclesiastes is fulfilled in Wisdom. Suffering is not without purpose. There *is* a final reward for virtue. Contrary to the teaching of Proverbs, that reward lies not only in material prosperity, but more completely in eternal life with God. Perhaps the first Deuteronomic teachers dimly foresaw the state of eternal happiness described in Wisdom, but were unable to find the concepts with which to express such a lofty vision. At any rate, with the Book of Wisdom, the Jewish understanding of Yahweh's response to good and evil had come of age. Along with the Book of Daniel, Wisdom gave the Jews a new theology of personal immortality, a theology which was to function as the final transfer point from the Old Testament to the New.

CHAPTER FIFTEEN

SHORT STORIES

**Ruth, Jonah, Esther,
Tobit, Judith**

There are five "short stories" in the Old Testament: Ruth, Jonah, Esther, Tobit and Judith.* Our modern short story is a much different genre than that represented by these five biblical books. Their underlying theological and didactic purpose makes them quite different from a story by O. Henry, Flannery O'Conner or Guy de Maupassant. Nevertheless, the term *short story* is probably the best label we can find to describe this type of biblical writing.

Each of these stories is concerned with the relationship between God's people and Gentiles. Several are written to assure the reader of Yahweh's superiority to pagan divinities and the religious supremacy of Yahweh's people over all the races of the earth. At the same time, however, the stories display either an underlying emphasis on Yahweh's compassion and mercy for non-Israelites or a conviction that Yahweh's actions embrace the lives of *all* peoples.

In four of the stories, women are either the chief character or play major roles. This emphasizes the theoretical social equality of all Israelites as well as the fact that charismatic leadership was a gift bestowed by Yahweh on persons otherwise ignored by then prevailing social hierarchies. The predominance of women, a powerless and disenfranchised group in Israelite society, emphasizes that it is Yahweh who is the deliverer, not mortal human beings. God's power works best

---

*Protestant Old Testaments exclude the latter two books in their entirety, and exclude as well the Greek portions of Esther.

in weakness (see 2 Cor 12:9). All but Jonah are concerned with one or more related themes: widowhood, the single state, marriage, remarriage, ancestry and family succession.

In these stories, then, we turn from wisdom literature's emphasis on the individual back to the traditional Jewish concern for the community. The thread which binds all of these stories together is the importance of the Israelites *as a people*.

Each of the five books recounts the story of some important communal tradition and how that tradition is subjected to peril—either of natural or human origin. Each story follows that threat to its point of greatest conflict—and then to resolution. Thus in each case the ongoing life of the community is enhanced. In each narrative Yahweh is present moving the events along, whether openly or secretly, toward a conclusion that preserves the integrity and well-being of his people as well as the integrity of his own name. Let us look briefly at each story.

RUTH

The Book of Ruth (Ru) comes from about the same time period as the composition of the Yahwist's epic—sometime between the 10th and eighth centuries B.C. Like the Yahwist, the author of Ruth was concerned with the Davidic ascendancy when he wrote this charming account of King David's Moabite great-grandmother, Ruth.

The plot revolves around the "levirate law" of Dt 25:5-10, which required the brother of a deceased married man to take his brother's widow as his own wife, in order to perpetuate the dead man's name. The story dramatizes for the reader the importance of the Law in Jewish tradition. The implication for the Jewish reader was this: If it weren't for the Law, there would have been no King David!

The Law is thus presented as completely supportive of Israelite family and community tradition. Keeping the Law is not only not a burden, it even brings great blessings. Here it saves two humble women—Naomi and Ruth—from destitution. The real hero of the story is the great lawgiver, Yahweh himself. His law is the means by which he blesses his people and prospers them. Without Yahweh's guiding hand, the central characters in the story would not have been able to turn misfortune into prosperity.

Ruth is the first piece of Israelite literature written about a woman who triumphs as a result of her own assertiveness. Ruth is the first "liberated woman" we will meet in these short stories. She and her later Israelite sisters saw their liberation as a means of making themselves available for greater service to the entire Israelite community. They also saw themselves as partners to men, complementing men's talents with their own and, through the wise use of their feminine virtues, enabling men to bring out the best of their masculine virtues.

As is brought out clearly in these five stories, the truly liberated human being is the person who maximizes his or her own talents through service of the community. Each of these stories is a story about personal freedom—and how that personal freeedom is fulfilled by using it for the greater good of the entire Israelite family. There are no better models today for true personal liberation than some of the figures portrayed in these five stories.

JONAH

Here the theme of personal liberation is displayed *in spite of* the often-humorous actions of the hero of the Book of Jonah (Jon). Written in postexilic times, possibly in the mid-fifth century B.C., this book stars an arch-traditionalist completely set in his ways. The thing Jonah feared most was an overturning of the status quo. In particular, Jonah didn't want anyone to tamper with his long-established picture of God.

To Jonah, Yahweh was the special possession of the Israelites. Furthermore Yahweh operated according to certain set formulas, one of which stated that good people prosper on account of their virtue and bad people suffer because of their wickedness. We saw this formula in operation before in considering D's theology, and we saw also the Old Testament's reaction to this type of thinking in Job.

The Book of Jonah is like the Book of Job in this respect: Both were written in reaction to the narrow, traditionalist viewpoint which equated prosperity with righteousness and suffering with wickedness. Jonah was also written in reaction to the exclusivist thinking prominent in the time of Nehemiah and Ezra.

In opposition to popular thought, the author of Jonah dared to write that Yahweh's mercy is universal. To dramatize this, he sets his story in the kingdom of the Assyrians—a people whose wickedness and cruelty were proverbial. The implication is that if Yahweh can forgive the Assyrians, he can forgive anybody. Conversely, if the Assyrians can avail themselves of Yahweh's mercy, anyone can.

The Book of Jonah is primarily theological in character, rather than historical. There *was* a prophet named Jonah but it is doubtful that he ever experienced any of the events described in the book bearing his name. Jonah, son of Amittai (2 Kgs 14:25), certainly didn't convert the Assyrians to Yahwism. Nor did anyone else for that matter. The Assyrians were perfectly horrid people right to the end of their history.

This acknowledgment of the historical inaccuracy of the Book of Jonah leads to one of the most popular questions about the entire Bible: "Did Jonah really get swallowed by a great fish?" My answer: probably not. Keep in mind that the author was writing religious fiction. And while anything is possible—particularly where God is in charge—the author of Jonah used the story about the fish for a different purpose than to demonstrate Yahweh's power over great sea creatures. His purpose was to show how one man experienced the utter deprivation of Yahweh's presence and through Yahweh's merciful salvation was brought to a new state of religious consciousness.

Jonah tried to flee from Yahweh, thinking that by escaping from him he would find freedom and independence. Yahweh had to show Jonah that human freedom is found only by submitting in trust to Yahweh's guidance and protection. Like the slaves Moses led from Egypt, Yahweh had to lead Jonah through a desert experience.

Unfortunately for the author, desert land was scarce in the middle of the Mediterranean. Therefore he had to find another means by which Yahweh could bring Jonah to a change of heart. Hence, the great fish. Jonah's transformation from man-relying-on-himself to man-dependent-on-Yahweh takes place in the belly of the fish. It was there that Yahweh lifted Jonah from the "pit" (2:7) of his own self-assurance to the liberation of his reliance on Yahweh.

The lesson Jonah learned in the belly of the fish was unfortunately forgotten as soon as he reached the city of Nineveh. In Nineveh Jonah was his old self—narrow-minded and prejudiced: He was outraged when Yahweh forgave the sins of the Ninevites.

Yahweh's free act of love and mercy flew in the face of Jonah's preconceived notion of how Yahweh *should* act. Yahweh then intervened to teach Jonah the true divine nature. Through the use of the castor-oil plant, Yahweh drove home the message that his love is universal and that Jonah's fellow human beings are of more importance in Yahweh's eyes than human traditions concerning divine retribution.

Jonah's reaction to Yahweh's forgiveness of the Ninevites reminds us of Elijah's reaction to Yahweh's defeat of Baal on Mt. Carmel. Both men grew angry that Yahweh did not follow through according to script. Jonah wanted Yahweh to destroy the wicked Ninevites and Elijah wanted Yahweh to stamp out Baalism in Israel for good. Yahweh did neither. The author of Jonah thus implies that Jonah's end would be like Elijah's: After a brief period of separation, Elijah came to know Yahweh even more intimately than before. If the story were to go on, my guess is that Jonah, too, would find his true identity—his true liberation—by accepting Yahweh's control over his life.

ESTHER

The next short story to appear in Old Testament times was the Book of Esther (Est). The Hebrew original of this work dates to about the late fourth century B.C. The remarkable thing about this work is that it nowhere mentions the word *God*! Perhaps as a reaction to this omission, later editors, writing in Greek, added a lot of "God-talk" to the Hebrew original, thus making it appear to be a more "spiritual" book than when it first appeared.

The *Jerusalem Bible* presents the Greek verses in italics. These Greek passages stand in clear contrast to the original Hebrew passages, which seem on first glance very secular in character. Since the Greek additions in a sense detract from the purpose of the original Hebrew author, we will not consider them here.

The author of the Hebrew passages in Esther made a daring departure from commonly-accepted Jewish literary norms. Traditional Jewish literature had always been careful to spell out humanity's insignificance before Yahweh and Yahweh's domination over the events of history. The author of Esther, by contrast, pushed Yahweh's control of events into the background and brought human ingenuity and independence into the foreground.

The principal Jewish characters in this book—Mordecai and Esther—succeeded through their own initiative, skill, cunning and bravado. Yahweh never intervened to help them—at least not openly. Thus Esther is very different from previous Jewish writings we have considered, in which we found Yahweh personally winning battles for his people or, at the very least, sending angels to assist his people in their struggles.

Because Esther is so human-centered, it barely made it into the Jewish canon of Scripture. Nevertheless Esther *is* there, giving us a remarkable teaching still very relevant today. That teaching revolves around the age-old question: How greatly does the devout believer rely on God, and how much on self?

The Book of Esther clearly tips the balance in favor of human activity. It was perhaps written in reaction to the supercilious piety of postexilic Jews who imagined that strict observance of the details of ritual, and nothing else, assured them of Yahweh's protection. This attitude is still with us. We see it, for example, among believers who pray earnestly for God to stamp out various social evils but do nothing to change society through active participation in the day-to-day struggle against injustice.

The message of Esther is clear: The devout believer is called to participate actively in the struggle against evil by confronting injustice and oppression openly, rather than waiting for God to win the battle by himself.

The teaching of Esther is not godless, however. Yahweh is nowhere mentioned by name, but he is nonetheless present—in the actions of loyal Jews who asserted themselves in favor of righteousness. Without mentioning Yahweh, the author demonstrates that Yahweh operated behind the scenes in Esther, stage-managing events so that Mordecai and Esther could triumph over the wicked Haman. Why else did King Ahasuerus suffer from insomnia precisely on that fateful night (Est 6)? Or was it simply a coincidence that Haman showed up at the very moment when the king decided to honor Mordecai for his loyalty?

The implication is obvious: Yahweh—while never mentioned by name—unobtrusively intervened on the side of his people, complementing their activity with his own. The message is that Yahweh helps those of his good and loyal people who help themselves. Yahweh does not regard his people as robots who are to sit around trance-like while he does all the work.

Esther thus sees human liberation coming to fulfillment only in the context of a partnership: God will do his part, but human beings must at the same time assert their own creativity in doing theirs.

TOBIT AND JUDITH

Our two final short stories, the Book of Tobit (Tb) and the Book of Judith (Jdt), repeat themes presented in Ruth and Esther. Like Ruth, Tobit is concerned with the sacredness of marriage and the preservation of family succession. Like Esther, Judith is concerned with the role a strong woman plays in saving her people from annihilation by a pagan power. Tobit is thus, like Ruth, a gentle book; while Judith, like Esther, leads to a violent climax.

Both books were written to assure Jews living under *Greek* domination of Yahweh's constant protection, although the setting of both books is the time of *Assyrian* domination, centuries before the books were written. Each book contains historical inaccuracies which in no way detract from the power of the books' respective teachings. Tobit is the earlier work, written about 200 B.C., while Judith was written a century or so later.

The more aggressive tone of Judith is due to the fact that the Maccabean-Seleucid struggle was in full bloom during the time of the book's composition. Judith is thus more militant than Tobit, more so even than Esther.

Tobit and Esther, like the first six chapters of Daniel, present a view of Jewish-Gentile relationship which allows for much accommodation between the two ways of life. Like the author of Dn 1—6, the authors of Tobit and Esther would permit Jewish integration into Gentile culture so long as Jews remained loyal to their faith. The author of Judith, on the other hand, presents the Gentiles as implacable enemies and sees no compromise possible between Jewish and Gentile ways.

Judith is the female version of *Judas*. The heroine of the book is thus presented as the female counterpart of the Maccabean hero, Judas. Like Judas Maccabaeus, Judith was a courageous warrior for Judaism, even though she subdued her enemy through subtlety and scheming rather than by battle.

Tobit, on the other hand, is a more traditional book in the sense that conservative D theology pervades much of it. In traditional fashion, an angel—Raphael—played a major role in the story. The author of Tobit broke little new ground and made no radical departure from traditional Jewish thought. As in Ruth, the importance of marrying within the family unit and preserving family continuity is the core of the Tobit story. Liberation, as seen by Tobit's author, takes place fully within the context of attunement to the Law. Tobit, Tobias and Sarah all submitted themselves to Yahweh's will as revealed in his Law.

When Tobias and Sarah married, they did so fully conscious they were participating in a greater event than simply their own union. They were fulfilling Yahweh's plan—revealed in the Law—through which his people were to continue their bonds of family and kin in perpetuity. Tobias and Sarah found the fulfillment of their individual interests in their concern for the overall interest of the community. Because of their righteousness, they removed the curses which had plagued their families. The demon who had killed Sarah's seven previous husbands was driven away and Tobit's sight was restored. As in our previous stories, the author places human liberation in the context of submission to Yahweh's will.

This theme is continued by the author of Judith. Like the central characters of the previous stories, Judith too was challenged by critical events to choose between her own interests and those of the community. Judith's choice was spontaneous: The community's interests took precedence over her own.

In no other short-story character in the Old Testament do we find a more harmonious blend of submissiveness to Yahweh and human assertiveness. Judith was a strong, dominant character, capable of making clear and immediate decisions. While the Jewish men in the story groveled in fear and confusion before the besieging Assyrians, Judith knew at once what she must do and set out boldly, without male assistance, to save the imperiled community.

Yet, she was not totally without assistance. She submitted her entire scheme to Yahweh, acknowledging him as the source of her strength and success:

> Please, please, God of my father,
> God of the heritage of Israel,
> Master of heaven and earth,
> Creator of the waters,
> King of your whole creation,
> hear my prayer.
> Give me a beguiling tongue
> to wound and kill
> those who have formed such cruel designs
> against your covenant,
> against your holy dwelling place,
> against Mount Zion,
> against the house belonging to your sons.
> And demonstrate to every nation, every tribe,
> that you are Yahweh, God almighty, all-powerful,
> and that the race of Israel
> has you for sole protector. (Jdt 9:12-14)

What a beautiful blend of submissiveness and assertiveness! Judith typifies true human liberation. She knew that Yahweh rules history, but that he does so only through human instruments who are willing to use their skills and talents in concert with him.

Judith avoided the two extremes of the spiritual life: She neither passively waited for Yahweh's miraculous intervention, nor charged ahead, self-assured and autonomous. She submitted her human talents to the will of Yahweh and asked him to use her talents for the common good of her people. That Yahweh did indeed use Judith in the story to preserve his people from annihilation demonstrates clearly for us today the Old Testament's conclusive message concerning the idea of human freedom.

CHAPTER SIXTEEN

THE PRAYER OF ISRAEL

Psalms

At the beginning of this book I said that in order to understand the Old Testament one must become at least a little bit Hebrew. By now it should be obvious why this is so. We have come to understand that the world of the Old Testament was a world very much different from our own. Unless we look at that world through the eyes of the Hebrews, we will miss the richness and depth which the Old Testament has to offer.

It is difficult for us today to imagine a society like Israel's which was principally religious in nature, rather than secular like our own. This religious character of ancient Israel is preserved for us in every book of the Old Testament, especially in that book which best summarizes Israel's religious spirit—the Book of Psalms (Ps).

Psalms is a collection of writings which records for us Israel's life as a worshiping community. The psalms thus preserve the deepest sentiments and emotions of a people involved in a love relationship with their God. To understand this people fully, we must be able to internalize some measure of the feeling which this relationship elicited in the lives of the Israelites. We do this by becoming absorbed in the spirit of the psalms.

Every love relationship calls for communication, and the Yahweh-Israel relationship was no exception. The psalms are the transcript of Israel's dialogue with Yahweh—a record of praise, thanksgiving, wonder, joy, struggles, doubts, fears and guilt. Without the psalms we would not have a complete picture of the people of the

Old Testament. We would not know them deeply as we do our own friends and loved ones.

Thus, if we really want to know this people and their sacred Scriptures intimately, we must pray and meditate on the psalms and allow these prayers to percolate into the depths of our own being. Then we will become a little bit Hebrew; then we will be in a position to know Israel's God as the Israelites themselves knew him and to participate in the love relationship with Yahweh which is the story of the Old Testament.

A love relationship is not a rational undertaking which one plans and accomplishes by willpower and effort. It is a spontaneous, emotional, often confusing and perplexing experience which sometimes leaves us feeling as though we have been on a roller coaster ride. This analogy will perhaps prepare us to read the psalms.

We will not find in the psalms any logical, well-planned scheme by which we are instructed to come to an intellectual understanding of God, only a wide variety of language and emotions—as one would expect to find in a dialogue between two lovers—which enables us to experience Yahweh as a *person*.

Sometimes this dialogue between Yahweh and his people is prudent and level-headed, as in the "wisdom psalms" (Ps 1, 32, 34, 37, 49, 112, 128). In these, Yahweh tells his people:

> I will instruct you, and teach you the way to go;
> I will watch over you and be your adviser. (Ps 32:8)

At other times the dialogue is joyous and exuberant, as in the "psalms of praise" (Ps 8, 19:1-7, 29, 33, 46—48, 65—66:12, 76, 77:14-21, 84, 87, 93, 95—99, 104, 111, 113—114, 117, 122, 129, 134—136, 139, 145—150). In these Israel spontaneously expresses the happiness and elation found in the relationship with Yahweh:

> Yahweh, our Lord,
> how great your name throughout the earth! (Ps 8:1)

> God, your ways are holy!
> What god so great as God? (Ps 77:13)

> Let heaven praise Yahweh:
> praise him, heavenly heights,
> praise him, all his angels,
> praise him, all his armies!
>
> Praise him, sun and moon,

praise him, shining stars,
praise him, highest heavens,
and waters above the heavens! (Ps 148:1-4)

Let everything that breathes praise Yahweh! (Ps 150:6)

At still other times in the relationship with Yahweh, Israel is depressed, angry, guilty, sad, frightened. The people know that with Yahweh they can be themselves; they turn to him in any mood and tell him their true feelings. The psalms which express these more somber feelings have been called "laments" (Ps 3—7, 10, 14 (53), 17, 22, 25—28, 35—36, 38—39, 40:12-18, 42—43, 51—52, 54—59, 61, 63—64, 69—71, 77:2-11, 86, 88, 102, 109, 120, 140—143). We find in these a wide variety of moods and a wide variety of petitions.

Yahweh, do not punish me in your rage,
or reprove me in the heat of anger.
Pity me, Yahweh, I have no strength left,
heal me, my bones are in torment.
Yahweh, how long will you be? (Ps 6:1-3)

Have mercy on me, O God, in your goodness,
in your great tenderness wipe away my faults;
wash me clean of my guilt,
purify me from my sin. (Ps 51:1-2)

The occasional anger and vindictiveness in these psalms of lament sometimes shock pious readers:

Down with them! Disgrace on those
who enjoy my misfortune!
May they be aghast with shame,
those who say to me, "Aha! Aha!" (Ps 70:3)

May Yahweh slice off every flattering lip,
each tongue so glib with boasts,
those who say, "In our tongue lies our strength,
our lips have the advantage; who can master us?" (Ps 12:3-4)

THE HONESTY OF THE PSALMS

Anyone raised on such religious sentiments as "love your enemies and pray for those who persecute you" (Mt 5:44) may have difficulty with this category of psalms. We should remember, however, that the psalms are, above all else, honest. If we examine our own lives we may find that we have more often wished to say, "God, *crush* my enemies!" than, "God, *heal* my enemies!"

The anger and vituperation in these psalms of lament are born of an honest relationship with God. While such sentiments may not always be pleasant, they nonetheless represent a necessary stage through which we all pass in getting to know God's ways more fully. Unless we can go to God with our true emotions, we will never be able to relate to him on a mature basis.

Praying these psalms of anger may at times be the most honest self-expression we can make. A humble admission of our own anger and frustration may lead us to a deeper understanding of God's ways. We may realize, like the psalmist, that God frequently uses our anger and hurt feelings to teach us more fully about his love for us. Notice the contrast between the psalmist's burst of anger in Ps 56:1-9 and his confident conclusion concerning Yahweh's protection:

> This I know: that God is on my side.
> In God whose word I praise....(Ps 56:10)

This brief smattering of psalms indicates the style and content of the writing found in the Book of Psalms. These psalms can help us non-Israelites attune ourselves to that deep experience of intimacy with Yahweh which the Israelites had. By praying the psalms regularly, we integrate ourselves more fully into Yahweh's worshiping community.

The starting point of that integration is our own consciousness. By allowing the psalms to reshape our thought patterns and our values, we will slowly be transformed from within. We will come to know Yahweh as Moses knew him, and as did Elijah, Jeremiah and David. We will be on intimate terms with the God of Abraham, Isaac and Jacob. Such an experience of Yahweh will mean that we, like Job, will be forever changed, ready to be led by Yahweh, ready to submit in love to Yahweh's call to us.

Through praying the psalms we will undergo a "spiritual revolution" so that we can "put on the new self that has been created in God's way, in the goodness and holiness of the truth" (Eph 4:24). The psalms, then, are to be used as a means of transforming our awareness, of changing our narrow, limited perspective into the very mind of Yahweh. By approaching the psalms in this way, we will come to that fullness of relationship with Yahweh which motivated the writers of Israel's sacred Scriptures. It is only in the context of this relationship that we truly come to an understanding of the Old Testament.

CONCLUSION

It was a dusty path that meandered from the marketplace of Nazareth to the squat old synagogue outside of town. A breathless young man hurried along the path on a hot summer day, anxious to make it to the synagogue for afternoon prayer. The Jews in the village observed the customary practice of praying in the morning, at noon and in the afternoon. The young man arrived a few minutes late.

Old Eleazar, the leader for the week, cocked an eyebrow and observed the late arrival. "Very unusual," he thought. "He's usually the first one here and the last to leave."

A few other men turned their heads as their townsman wrapped himself in his *tallith*—prayer shawl—and moved toward a seat.

The congregation had already completed the great *Shema!* and had paused before beginning its next round of prayers. As in all synagogues in Palestine, the men faced Jerusalem as they prayed. Slowly Eleazar began to intone the words to the first psalm of the afternoon. The rest of the men followed his lead:

> Yahweh my God, I take shelter in you;
> from all who hound me, save me, rescue me....(Ps 7:1)

Eleazar noticed old Phineas dozing in the back row. He motioned toward the man who had just arrived and moved his elbow back and forth a few times, as if to say, "Jab him one, will you?"

The man walked over to Phineas, who by this time was snoring loudly, and touched him on the shoulder. Phineas jumped up and mumbled:

> Yahweh is my shepherd,
>   I lack nothing.
> In meadows of green grass he—(Ps 23:1-2)

Eleazar was grimacing and waving his arms while the other men kept singing the correct psalm. Two boys snickered and then laughed out loud. Eleazar shook his finger at them.

The first psalm finished, Eleazar motioned for Rabbi Jacob to start another. Jacob had a deep voice and loved to lead the singing. He began,

> Shout for joy to Yahweh, all virtuous men,
> praise comes well from upright hearts....(Ps 33:1)

This one went much better. Everyone seemed to concentrate, even the two boys in the back. This psalm and another completed, the men took up the *Shemoneh Esreh,* the "Eighteen Benedictions." They bowed deeply and piously at appropriate moments as the long, repetitious litany continued.

The service was drawing to a close. "Some reading from the Scriptures and a brief teaching would make a nice conclusion," Eleazar thought. "Whom will I select?"

He surveyed his little flock. Each man stared down at the ground, knowing why Eleazar was looking them over. Each man but one, that is. The late arrival was looking eagerly at the leader. One could almost see the question written on his face: "May I read today, Master?"

Eleazar loved the young man—indeed, the entire congregation did. There was no one more devout, more pious, no one who was a better Jew.

"How can I refuse?" the old man thought. "This fellow is a blessing for us all. Still, I wonder if he's not too intense. He is as devoted to Yahweh as was David himself. Is that kind of attitude healthy? Oh, well, no one else seems interested."

The young man eagerly accepted Eleazar's nod of invitation. Rabbi Jacob and another man handed him a scroll, and the young man began to read:

> The spirit of the Lord Yahweh has been given to me,
> for Yahweh has anointed me.

He has sent me to bring good news to the poor,
to bind up hearts that are broken....(Is 61:1)

The congregation was spellbound. They had heard him read before, but this time his earnestness and emotion filled the room like crackling rays of lightning. No one stirred when he had finished. Then, lifting up his head and looking around the room at the men, he said,

"This day these words have been fulfilled in your presence." (See Lk 4:21)

A FINAL PLEA

This concludes our inquiry into the story behind the writing of the Old Testament. We have seen how these varied and multi-faceted books came into being within the life experience of the Hebrew people. We have seen also that the Old Testament is the record of the love affair between a people and their God.

What does that record have to say to us today? Is the Old Testament a dead transcript of events which has no relevance to modern times? Or is there a timeless element in the story which speaks with great force to humanity on the brink of the 21st century?

We will find the answer to that question only by approaching the Old Testament in the same way that the psalmist approached his daily prayer—by seeking to know the face of the living God. Studies of Scripture such as this one are helpful to lead us to knowledge *about* the Word of God, but really to *know* the Word of God as the psalmist did, we must pick up the Old Testament in the same prayerful spirit which moved the psalmist.

To understand the Old Testament, we must acknowledge that yearning deep within ourselves for intimate knowledge of the only One who can still our restlessness and bring us to fulfillment. We will be able to know the relevance of the Old Testament in our lives only when we can say, with the psalmist,

As a doe longs
for running streams,
so longs my soul
for you, my God. (Ps 42:1)

The conclusion of this book is thus a plea—a plea for the reader to get to know the Old Testament from the inside out, by reading it daily in a spirit of receptivity and yearning:

•Cross the Sea of Reeds with your ancestors in faith.

•Stand at the foot of Mt. Sinai with Moses as Yahweh calls you to become a member of his consecrated nation.

•Learn from the desert experience of the Hebrew nomads as you walk through your own daily desert.

•Rejoice before the Lord and accept the refreshment of his forgiveness as David did.

•Sense the strength which comes from devotion to Yahweh's Law, as experienced in the lives of Ruth, Esther and Judith.

•Like Job, surrender to the mystery of Yahweh's power and majesty.

•If necessary, vent your anger at Yahweh like Jeremiah or declare to him that you "have had enough" as did Elijah.

In short, recreate the pages of the Old Testament in your own consciousness. This study should have given you ample suggestions on how to begin. Follow your own preferences. If you're the active type, you may want to start with a passage from 1 Kings. Or if you're more introspective, Proverbs or Sirach may be a better beginning point for you.

Wherever you start, keep at it. Come back each day in a spirit of adventure, quest and challenge. It won't be long before you will know the answer to the questions above concerning the relevance of the Old Testament to modern times:

> Yes, if your plea is for clear perception,
>> if you cry out for discernment,
> if you look for it as if it were silver,
>> and search for it as for buried treasure,
> you will then understand what the fear of Yahweh is,
>> and discover the knowledge of God. (Prv 2:3-5)

Enjoy your adventure!

171

INDEX